The CHRISTMAS PROMISE

TEACHING MATERIAL FOR 3-5S, 5-8S AND 8-12S

thegoodbook for children

The Christmas Promise Sunday School Lessons
© The Good Book Company, 2023.

Lessons written by Lizzie Laferton. Prepare Your Heart sections written by Carl Laferton. Based on the storybook by Alison Mitchell.

Published by:
The Good Book Company

thegoodbook.com | thegoodbook.co.uk
thegoodbook.com.au | thegoodbook.co.nz | thegoodbook.co.in

ISBN: 9781784989026 | JOB-007293 | Printed in India

Design by André Parker | Illustrations from *The Christmas Promise* storybook by Catalina Echeverri

Contents

Introduction

Welcome to this adventure in God's Christmas promises!

In this three-lesson series for 3-12-year-olds, the children you teach will trace the message of God's promised King from his foretelling in Isaiah to his Christmas arrival. The series follows the structure of the best-selling storybook *The Christmas Promise* and is intended to help children to dig deeper into Bible passages from Isaiah, Matthew and Luke that underpin it.

Each of the three sessions in the series includes:

- a "Prepare Your Heart" section, helping you to enjoy and apply the truths yourself, before you teach them to your children's group.

- a lesson plan for 3-5-year-olds.

- a lesson plan for 5-12-year-olds, with different Bible-time questions and activities signalled as being for "Younger Children" (approximately 5-7-year-olds) and "Older Children" (approximately 8-12-year-olds). These teach directly from the Bible to examine God's promises about his forever, rescuing King in Isaiah and see their fulfilment in the New Testament.

- free, downloadable PDFs containing the relevant Bible passages, questions, activity sheets, and resources for certain activities, games and crafts for you to use with your group, as well as downloads of all the illustrations from the storybook. (You will see the icon to the right wherever the session is talking about something that is included in the download.)

The lesson overviews below give more details on exactly what the lesson plans for the different age groups include.

The resource also includes an outline and suggested detail for an all-age service that shares what the children have been discovering about the promised King. It recaps the promises in Isaiah and elements of the Christmas narrative the children have seen, and invites people to consider and emulate the responses of Mary, the shepherds and the wise men to Jesus, God's promised King.

We have put each lesson together in a way that means you can deliver it exactly as it's written: all activities, scripts, Bible studies, questions, links and prayers are provided for every session, as well as games and craft ideas. (Please note that you'll need a copy of the storybook for teaching a 3-5s group.) If preparation time is pressed, or you are new to teaching children, we want to give as much support as possible. At the start of each session for 5-12s, we've also included an outline of the aims of each part of the session, making it easy for you to adapt things to suit your particular group.

ⓘ *Where you see a text marked in this way in the 5-12s' plan, it's a note for you as the leader, rather than something intended to be read aloud to the group!*

Having bought this book, you now have access to free, downloadable material. You can download the content of this book as a PDF, for free, as many times as you like, to share with other leaders and helpers within your church. (Please note that you are not allowed to share it more widely outside your own church.) You'll find all the downloadable material at **thegoodbook.com/ tcplessonresources**, and will need to enter the passcode at the top of the next page.

The scripts and Bible studies use the International Children's Bible (ICB), New International Reader's Version (NIRV), New Living Translation (NLT) and New International Version (NIV). They will work with other translations, but we recommend aiming to use translations with simpler sentence structures, especially for the Bible studies where older children are being asked to find answers from the text themselves with less support. Memory verses are from the New International Version.

If You're Teaching 3-5-year-olds...

Session Structure

Each of the three lesson plans contains a number of segments that can be adapted for your circumstances.

The core elements of each lesson are:

1)*   A short opening prayer

2)   Reading the relevant pages from *The Christmas Promise*

5)   A simple statement summarising that section's teaching (See the "God's Word Tells Us..." summary in each lesson plan)

6)   Sharing a Bible verse that shows that the truths in the book come from the Bible

7)   A simple closing prayer

* The numbers here correspond to numbered segments in the full lesson plans provided.

In addition, you can include any/all of the following optional elements:

3)   Simple questions that engage with the book reading

4)   A game that reinforces the teaching point as well as providing movement and a concentration break

8)   A craft activity that reinforces the teaching point

Sample explanations are also included for how to show the children the link between the game/craft and what they have been learning.

Series Overview

SESSION	MAIN TEACHING POINT
1. The Forever King	Jesus is God's promised forever King. He will always look after his people.
2. The Rescuing King	Jesus is God's promised rescuing King. He is great news! Note: During this session, you may want to explain to the children what "sin" is in an age-appropriate way. Here is one suggestion for how you could do so: "Sin is not loving God, not listening to God, and not letting God be in charge".
3. The New King	Jesus is God's promised new King. Jesus is King for all sorts of people everywhere.
Family Service	God promised to send a King who is different to all other kings. Jesus is that King. He is the new, rescuing, forever King. Mary, the shepherds and the wise men show us what it looks like when we treat Jesus as our King.

If You're Teaching 5-12-year-olds...

Session Structure

For each of the parts of the session outlined below, the lesson plans provide examples and ideas. Each full session plan also begins with an individual lesson outline going into more detail on the goals of each segment for that particular session.

Each session includes:

SESSION ELEMENT	PURPOSE
Recap	Provide a brief review of previous sessions.
Introductory Activity	Introduce or set up an idea that will help the children understand the Bible ideas and/or apply the truths they will think about.
Opening Prayer	Model prayer seeking God's help to understand and act on his word.

Bible Teaching	This first Bible-teaching section is intended to be the briefer of the two. It involves a brief discussion of a few verses from Isaiah.

In each lesson there are two different suggested studies, one for younger and one for older children. If you have the full age range in your class, these could be done in separate groups before you come together for the closing summary statement.

Studies for younger children do not require them to read, and involve a variety of activities to help them engage with and understand the passage. Studies for older children require them to do more close textual work and articulate their understanding for themselves.

The age ranges suggested are just a guide, and you may want to modify or combine ideas for your particular children. |
| Game | Different ideas are given for games that allow an opportunity to move about / take a break in concentration, but which also reinforce or set up a teaching point. |
| Bible Teaching | This second Bible-teaching section involves the leader telling and explaining the parts of the birth narrative of Christ that reveal that God was fulfilling the promises made through Isaiah.

Example scripts are provided that tell and explain the relevant part of Luke or Matthew using a mixture of Bible verses from various translations, paraphrased storytelling and interactive question-and-answer segments. The lesson plans also provide suggestions for how to engage the children visually or with movement in the storytelling. |
Application	Depending on the session, this will involve a very short talk from the teacher or whole-group discussion or pair work or an opportunity to think individually. The aim is to encourage the children to consider what difference the truths you have been learning about make to our lives today.
Prayer	Model or give opportunities for responding to God and his word in prayer. Various suggestions for what this might involve are given, ranging from very supported/scaffolded to more open times of prayer.
Craft/Activities	An opportunity to exercise some God-given creativity and enjoy a reminder of the lesson! Various suggestions are given, ranging from those requiring pen and paper to crafts that need some minimal resourcing to more time/ resource-heavy and/or complex projects.
At Home	Encourage families to keep thinking and praying together during the week about what the children have learnt at church. Suggestions are given for resources and ideas that could be shared with parents.

Series Overview

SESSION	GOD'S WORD TELLS US...	SO WHAT?	BIBLE PASSAGES
1. The Forever King	God promised to send a King unlike any other. Jesus is that King. There is no limit to the length of his righteous reign—he will be all-powerful and always perfect for all time.	The good news is that Jesus is the best ruler we could ever hope for. A right response is to joyfully entrust ourselves to his good rule.	Isaiah 9 v 6-7; Luke 1 v 26-38
2. The Rescuing King	God promised to send a King who would rescue his people from sin. Jesus is that King. There is no limit to the lengths he will go to—he is the good Shepherd who lays down his life for his sheep.	The good news is that Jesus transforms fear of judgment into joy and peace with God. A right response is to praise him and share the good news of who he is.	Isaiah 53 v 4-6; Luke 2 v 1-20
3. The New King	God promised to send a new type of king who would be for all types of people. Jesus is that King. There is no limit to the extent of his rule—he is the rescuing, forever King for people from every tribe, tongue and nation.	The good news is that Jesus welcomes all sorts of people from all over the world into his kingdom. A right response is to accept that invitation by recognising and worshipping him as our King.	Isaiah 49 v 5-7; Matthew 2 v 1-12

| Family Service | God promised to send a King unlike any other. Jesus is that King. He is the new, rescuing, forever King.

He is the best ruler we could ever hope for: he will be all-powerful and always perfect for all time; he is the good Shepherd who lays down his life for his sheep; and he is all this for people from every tribe, tongue and nation. | The good news is that Jesus is the King we can trust for forgiveness and entrust ourselves to. He is the King we can access and come to, whoever we are. He is a King worthy of being sought and celebrated and shared and worshipped.

A right response to him will involve coming to him, as the shepherds did, acknowledging his right to rule, as the wise men did, and trust in him, as Mary did. | Isaiah 9 v 6-7; 49 v 6-7; 53 v 5-6 |

SESSION 1
The Forever King

The Forever King – Prepare Your Heart

 Read Luke 1 v 26-38

- What do these verses tell us about Mary's baby?

- What does verse 37 tell us about God's word/promises? What does verse 38 show us is the right response to this truth?

Here is one of the most familiar parts of one of the most familiar stories in the entire Western world—and so there's a danger that familiarity dims the glory and the surprise of it. So, as you prepare your heart to teach the children in your group, here are three truths about the God who lies behind all the events of Christmas—and who came to lie at the centre of Christmas.

First, he is a *surprising* God. When he sends his angel Gabriel to make this world-changing announcement, it's not to a political centre such as Rome or a religious centre such as Jerusalem. Instead it's to a backwater town so unremarkable that it is not mentioned even once in the entire Old Testament—Nazareth. Not only that, but the announcement was not for a leader, or a priest, but an unmarried girl (probably a teenager)—Mary. If we were God, we wouldn't have done it like this! But as the old hymn puts it, God moves in mysterious ways his wonders to perform. So the first Christmas should prompt us to be open to God surprising us—to read his word ready to have our hearts and minds changed by what he says there, and to head through our days looking for God to be working in us and around us in ways we hadn't expected and perhaps cannot explain.

Second, he is a *present* God. The angel's message is that God himself, God the Son, is going to grow as a human in a womb and live as a human in his own world. The most amazing thing is not that this is a virgin birth but that it is a divine birth (v 35). Why is the divine stepping into history? To rule. He is a King (v 32) who will

reign over "Jacob's descendants" (v 33)—the promised king, the Messiah (or "Christ"), descended from David and fulfilling all the prophecies of the Old Testament. Not only that, but his kingdom will never end. Here is a forever King—a King powerful enough to keep his promises and eternal enough to keep his promises. However great (or not) the ruler of your nation is, and however great (or not) the next one will be, they will not be perfect and they will not endure. Whether by death, overthrow or democratic vote, they will leave office. Jesus is a different kind of ruler. He never disappoints, never makes a mistake, never acts selfishly and never leaves his throne. He is the perfect forever King.

And third, therefore, here is a God who is *worthy of our joyful service*—even when that's costly. Mary faced losing her impending marriage, her reputation, her hopes and dreams. She didn't know it, but she would face watching her son die. Yet she responded, "I am the Lord's servant … May your word to me be fulfilled" (v 38). She said yes, because she trusted God and so was willing to be part of his plan. Serving God is sometimes painful, but it is always a privilege—for us just as for Mary. We will not bear God's Son, but we are called to serve him and be part of his plans for his world. What else would we want to spend our lives doing?! And who else would we entrust ourselves to?! Perhaps this Christmas would be a good time to say to King Jesus, "I am your servant. I trust you. I'm all yours."

- Look back over the past year. In what surprising ways have you seen God at work in your life or in the lives of others?

- What areas of service has God called you to? In what ways are those costly? What causes for joy have they given you, and how does reflecting on those help you to say "King Jesus, I'm all yours"?

God's Word Tells Us...
Jesus is God's promised forever King. He will always look after his people.

🙏 1. Pray
Let's talk to God before we read the story:

Dear God, please show us why Jesus is the best King ever. Amen.

👂 2. Listen
Read *The Christmas Promise* storybook from the beginning up to and including the page spread that looks like this...

To make the reading interactive, you could:

- look at the pictures on the first double-page spread and ask them the names of any famous kings or queens, presidents or prime ministers they've heard of. Or ask them where they might see a picture of a king or queen or ruler (in history books, on TV, on coins and notes, on stamps, on playing cards). You could have examples of these items to show them.

- ask how we might know if someone is a king/queen and have props for dressing a child up in a crown and a robe and then seat them on a "throne".

- point to the picture of the castle on the first double-page spread and ask them what they think it might be like inside. When you get to the picture of Mary's home, before reading the text, ask them if it looks like the sort of place they imagine a king living. Why/why not?

- tell them to do an action such as putting on a crown every time they hear the word "king".

☁️ 3. Thinking
- Who promised to send a King who would be different from all other kings and queens?

- Did God keep that promise by sending Jesus?

- Is Jesus special because he is going to be King for ever?

🏁 4. Game
"How long can you...?" Give the children simple physical challenges and ask them if they think they can keep going without stopping for 5 seconds, 10 seconds, 30 seconds, a minute, two minutes, five minutes...! Have fun seeing how long they can stand on one leg, run on the spot, do star jumps, spin in a circle, and so on, before they tire or topple!

Then say:

"We can't do things for ever, but Jesus can! Jesus is the King who is going to be king for ever."

OR

"How long will it last?" Have various easily breakable/tear-able items in a bag. Invite children one at a time to pick something out of the bag and have a go at breaking it. Items might include a breadstick, a rice cake, a piece of dried lasagne/spaghetti, a piece of paper, a biscuit, some dried cereal, a cardboard tube… Once the final one has been removed, sneak a coin into the bag and ask a child to pull it out and have a go at breaking it. Encourage them to stamp on it or (safely!) hit it with something.

Then say:

"Lots of things break. Things don't last for ever. But the coin is more like Jesus: Jesus is strong. Jesus will be there for ever. Jesus will be a strong King for ever."

5. Summary Statement

Jesus is the King who God promised. Jesus will be King for ever.

6. Listen to God from the Bible

We know this because in Luke chapter 1 verse 33 the Bible tells us that Jesus "will rule forever over his people" (NIRV).

7. Pray

Let's talk to God again now:

Lord Jesus, you are the King who will be in charge for ever. You will never change or stop loving us. Wow! Amen.

8. Craft Ideas

- Give the children the colouring page of Mary and the angel from the activity book for them to colour/stick on household items (see downloadable sheet).

- Give each child a paper or card crown with "JESUS is the FOREVER King" on it. They can decorate it with pens/stickers/tissue paper/craft jewels etc. before you tape/staple it to fit them.

- Make paper-plate or cardboard-tube angels. (There are lots of simple ideas for how to do these on the internet.) Prepare speech bubbles containing the words "Jesus is God's promised forever King" for children to stick on.

- As the children enjoy crafting, you could ask them what makes Jesus different from other kings. What made him different from other babies?!

God's Word Tells Us...

God promised to send a King unlike any other. Jesus is that King. There is no limit to the length of his righteous reign—he will be all-powerful and always perfect for all time.

So What?

The good news is that Jesus is the best ruler we could ever hope for. A right response is to joyfully entrust ourselves to his good rule.

SECTION	PURPOSE	SUGGESTED ACTIVITY
Let's Get Ready Introduction	Establish that no earthly rulers rule perfectly and none last forever. Introduce series aim: to look at God's promise to send a King who would be unlike any other.	Brief discussion of the children's answers to an opening question about famous historical rulers.
Opening prayer	Pray for the session.	
Let's Hear God's Promise Bible teaching and discussion	Show that the King God promised to send would be God himself and that he would rule perfectly and for ever. He would be unlike any other ruler there has ever been.	Age-appropriate discussion or Bible study of Isaiah 9 v 6-7. Both could be done in smaller groups. Note: This section is intended to be a shorter Bible teaching segment than the second one.

	Let's Play a Game	Provide a break for concentration. Reinforce the idea that normal rulers don't last forever OR that normal rulers have weaknesses as well as strengths. Jesus is unlike other rulers.	Two game options depending on time / space limitations.
	Let's See God's Promise Kept Bible teaching and discussion	Show from Luke 1 that God kept his promise by sending Jesus: Jesus is the forever King whom God promised in Isaiah 9. He is unlike any other king because he is God himself.	Tell the story of Gabriel's visit to Mary using Bible verses and interactive storytelling, and involving actors and/or props if possible, drawing out the significance of what the angel says. An example of what this might involve is given below and can be adapted to suit your age group and/or resources.
	What Does This Mean for Us? Application	Discuss what makes Jesus the best possible ruler. Consider what a right response to Jesus—the perfect, forever King—involves, using Mary's example.	Group discussion and guided questions for use as a whole class or in smaller groups.
	Let's Talk to God about That Prayer	Give opportunities to praise our promise-making, promise-keeping Father, and Christ, the perfect, forever King.	A number of different options depending on the circumstances of the group.
	Let's Get Creative Reinforcement	Enjoy an activity together that picks up on an element of the story, giving time for conversation with the children to hear their thoughts about what they've learned.	Craft activities: Various options requiring different levels of resourcing.
	At Home	Provide ways for families to continue thinking together about the wonder of God's promised forever King.	Various possible activities that pick up on/reinforce this session.

 **Let's Get Ready**

… by thinking about some famous rulers.

ⓘ *Put children in pairs or small groups.*

Here are six pictures of famous rulers from around the world and throughout history.

- In your pairs/groups, I want you to try to name as many of them as you can and see if you can think of one thing they are famous for.

ⓘ *Display pictures/portraits of six monarchs and/or national rulers you think the children are likely to recognise and know a little about. This will depend on your country and context (and possibly school curriculum!), but here are some suggestions: Elizabeth II, Queen Victoria, Henry VIII, Winston Churchill, Margaret Thatcher, Nelson Mandela, Cleopatra, Julius Caesar, Abraham Lincoln, George Washington, Barack Obama. If you have a range of ages in your class, spread older children through the groups. You will need to know how long each person ruled for. For younger children you might have facts already prepared for the children to match to a picture, for instance: "Which king is famous for having six wives?"*

- What can you tell me about each person? / Which ruler is famous for…?

- Which of them do you think ruled for the most time? Who do you think ruled for the least?

Throughout history there have been famous rulers—kings and queens, presidents and prime ministers. Some of them ruled for many decades. Some ruled for only a few years. Some ruled just for months, weeks or even days! Some of them are famous for great deeds and good character. Some of them are famous for what terrible rulers they were. But as we look back over history we see one ruler after another after another. Rulers come and rulers go, because no king or queen lives forever!

BUT, long ago, God made a promise. He promised to send a King who would be unlike any other ruler there has ever been. The Old Testament—the first part of the Bible—is full of details about God's promised King. Lots of them are found in the book of Isaiah.

Over the next few weeks, we're going to look at some of those promises in Isaiah to discover what this promised King is like. And we're going to look at the Christmas story in the New Testament to see how God kept his promise at the first Christmas.

 Let's Pray

… before we start.

Mighty, everlasting Father, please excite us about your promised King and show us why he is so much better than other rulers. Amen.

So, what was different about God's promised King?

Let's Hear God's Promise

… that God gave to his people through his messenger, a man called Isaiah.

 (i) *The tasks below are based on the ICB version and may need to be adapted. Share the tasks among your group. Give each task (and especially the "name" activity) to multiple children where possible. Downloadable resources are provided that you can use for visual support. You will need to print and cut the pictures ahead of time and have means of sticking them up somewhere.*

For Younger Children

I am going to read two verses from a promise God made through his messenger Isaiah. God promised to send a special child. As I read it…

- you need to listen out for at least one NAME this child will be known by. (If you can remember two, three or even four, that's amazing!)

- you need to listen out for a word beginning with the letter/sound "p" that gets said twice.

- you need to listen out for any words that mean the same as "mighty".

- you need to listen out for a word that means the opposite of evil.

- you need to listen out for a word that means the opposite of unfair.

- you need to listen out for how long he will be king for.

(i) *Read Isaiah 9 v 6-7 slowly and clearly, emphasising key words.*

If you're using the pictures provided, stick up the picture of the baby. As you ask the relevant children/groups the following questions, stick up the relevant pictures to summarise the different facts they pull out about the promised King.

- What names for this child did you hear? *(Wonderful Counsellor, Powerful God, Father who Lives For Ever, Prince of Peace)*

(i) *Stick the crown over the baby's head.*

God promised to send a child who would be a Prince, a King. God promised to send a child who would be God himself!

- What word beginning with "p" gets said twice? *(Peace)*

(i) *Stick up the smiley face.*

- What word did you hear that means the same as "mighty"? *(Powerful)*

(i) *Stick up the strong arm.*

- What word did you hear that means the opposite of evil? *(Goodness)*

(i) *Stick up the heart.*

- What word did you hear that means the opposite of unfair, or unjust? *(Fair)*

(i) *Stick up the big tick/check mark.*

- God promised that this King's reign would be powerful, always good, always fair and full of peace. Does that sound to you like a good kingdom to live in or a bad kingdom to live in?

- How long did Isaiah say this King would be king for? *(For ever / for ever and ever)*

ⓘ *Stick up the arrow.*

God promised a King unlike any other. God promised a King who would rule powerfully and perfectly. Other rulers have some power. Other rulers rule well sometimes. But none are all-powerful. None are always perfect. And even when they're doing an ok job of ruling, none of them are everlasting! But the King God promised is all those things. And he is all those things because he IS God himself. God promised that HE was going to come into the world to be the forever King—to be God with us.

For Older Children

ⓘ *Give older children a copy of the biographical details card to fill in based on Isaiah 9 v 6-7. You could divide the categories among the group if time is short. They read the verses and pick out the names from v 6, the characteristics of his rule from v 7, and the length of his reign.*

Once they have picked out that information and you have discussed the answers, ask:

- What do those names reveal about this King? *(Possible answers include: he is God himself; he will bring supernatural wisdom; he is powerful and eternal; he is loving—a Father; he brings peace.)*

- What sounds appealing about living in his kingdom? *(Possible answers: there will be peace, justice/fairness and righteousness/goodness; those things will never end—nothing will spoil them; there'll be no fear of change / of things getting spoiled; he will be powerful, so he can protect his people and give them what they need.)*

- What makes him different from all other kings and rulers? *(Possible answers: he is always good and always fair; his rule won't feature evil or injustice; he will reign forever—he won't leave us or let us down; his rule won't feature uncertainty or doubt or upheaval.)*

God promised a King unlike any other. God promised a King who would rule powerfully and perfectly. Other rulers have some power. Other rulers rule well sometimes. But none are all-powerful. None are always perfect. And even when they're doing an ok job of ruling, none of them are everlasting! But the King God promised is all those things. And he is all those things because he IS God himself. God promised that HE was going to come into the world to be the forever King—to be God with us.

🏁 Let's Play a Game

OPTION 1

ⓘ *An active game that picks up on the idea that kings come and go. Depending on space/numbers, you could play various four-player games on separate grids simultaneously. Play for a set amount of time. The winner is whoever is occupying the top position at the end of the time.*

Four Square/King Square: in a grid of four squares marked out with cones/tape, one child occupies each square. (An internet image search for "four square game" or "king square game" brings up results showing the game being played, to give an idea of scale for your grid.) One square is the King square and the aim of the game is to hold that position. The other three squares are successively "lower" such that one is the "bottom" square. The player in the King square serves a tennis ball or similar by bouncing it in their own square before hitting it with their hand into another square. Play continues with players hitting the ball into an opponent's square before it bounces a second time in their own and without bouncing it outside the grid. If they make either mistake, they go to occupy the lowest square (or are out and a new player takes the lowest square), with everyone else moving up one as appropriate. The winner is the one holding the King square when time is up.

In that game, the king could be knocked off the top spot. It's the same in real life—rulers come and go. So one thing that is so amazing about God's promised King is that he will be King for ever. There is no better king who could replace him.

OPTION 2

ⓘ *A less active game, appropriate for children who can read. Borrow various Top Trumps sets for the children to play with in small groups. If you can get hold of sets that are about rulers, even better! The children play in small groups for the length of time you decide.*

All of the animals/tractors/rulers/characters/trains etc. on your cards had different strengths and weaknesses. Some scored really highly for lots of things. Most had at least one category they were less strong in. If God's promised King had a "Top Trump" card he would score 100% for power, 100% for perfection and "for ever" for the length of his rule! God's promised King really is unlike any other ruler!

Let's Hear from God

We're going to hear from God as we read part of the New Testament now. The first four books of the New Testament were written by people who had either known Jesus when he was on earth or who had spoken with people who had. In Luke's account of Jesus' life, death and resurrection, Luke includes information he'd investigated about Jesus' birth. And in those true stories, we see lots of ways God showed everyone that he was keeping his promise.

ⓘ *Think about ways you can include visuals and/or movement in your New Testament storytelling, especially for younger children. For instance, pictures for different stages of the story; toy figures for the characters; a puppet theatre; a props box for you to pull relevant objects/clothes out of; leaders dressed up and acting the passage; children moving around the room to different "scenes" as the characters in the story do likewise.*

The Luke 1 passage is relatively static and unvaried, so leaders dressed up to deliver the lines might be the best option for this passage. The sample script below is based on the ICB and NIRV translations. Older children who can be relied on to read slowly and clearly could deliver the lines of the angel and Mary if given a script, and a fellow leader could be the narrator. At various points, the action is paused ("Freeze frame!") for comments or whole-group discussion to help draw out the significance of the passage. Some vocabulary has been paraphrased to help understanding and to avoid potential distractions (for instance "What is a virgin?").

Luke chapter 1 tells us that…

 Narrator: God sent the angel Gabriel to a girl who lived in Nazareth, a town in Galilee. She was engaged to marry a man named Joseph from the family of David. Her name was Mary. The angel came to her and said, "Greetings! The Lord has blessed you and is with you."

- Freeze frame! How would you feel if an angel showed up suddenly to talk to you? What would you wonder if the angel said to you, "The Lord has blessed you and is with you"?!

Well, if you wonder what that means, you're in good company… Action!

Narrator: Mary was very confused by what the angel said. Mary wondered,

Mary: What does this mean?

Narrator: The angel said to her…

Angel: Don't be afraid, Mary… Listen! You will become pregnant. You will give birth to a son, and you will name him Jesus.

- Freeze frame! Who was responsible for spotting names in our Isaiah passage? / Who can remember any names from our Isaiah passage? Please can you get ready to spot another name for Mary's son in the next bit of our story.

- Who was responsible for noticing things about the King and his rule? / Who can remember what Isaiah said about the promised King's kingdom? Please can you get ready to spot a word beginning with "g" that describes Mary's son.

- Who was responsible for spotting / Who can remember how long the promised King was going to rule for? Please get ready to spot what the angel says about Mary's son.

Action!

Angel: Jesus will be great, and people will call him the Son of the Most High. The Lord God will give him the throne of King David, his family member from long ago. Jesus will rule over his people for ever. His kingdom will never end.

- Freeze frame! What did the angel say Jesus would be like? What did he say Jesus would be called? How long will Jesus rule for?

Hurray! God's promised King has arrived! This is no ordinary King. AND this is no ordinary baby, as we're about to see…

Action!

Narrator: Mary said to the angel…

Mary: How will this happen? It's impossible for me to be pregnant.

Narrator: The angel said to Mary…

Angel: The Holy Spirit will come to you. The power of the Most High God will cover you. So the baby will be holy. He will be called the Son of God. God can do anything!

- Freeze frame! Jesus is like no other king because he is a human like no other human. Jesus' beginning on earth was unique. He was made by God's power through the Holy Spirit. Jesus is like no other king, and he is like no other baby, because Jesus is God the Son.

A round of applause for our actors, please!

◯ **What Does This Mean for Us?**

> ⓘ *You could do these questions as a think-pair-share activity where children have a short time to think, a moment to share ideas with someone, and then a chance to feed back to the wider group.*

At the beginning of the session we were thinking about the sort of people who rule our countries.

- Why is Jesus better than every other ruler there has ever been?

Jesus is the promised all-powerful King. Jesus is the promised always-perfect King. Jesus is the promised always-and-forever King.

- How do you think we should we treat a perfect ruler like that?

At the end of the true story we just heard, Mary gave us a good example of how to respond. The angel had just told her something life-changing. He had just told her something other people might not believe. He had just told her something that was amazing and mind-blowing and maybe a little bit scary.

But instead of worrying or doubting or trying to work out what to do next, Mary simply said… wait for it… "I am the Lord's servant. Let this happen to me as you say!" Wow!

- What word would you use to sum up her response?

For Younger Children

- Let's think about what Mary is saying about God. How might Mary finish this sentence? *(Do as think-pair-share.)*

The Lord God is my _____. I will trust him to _____ my life.

Answers might include: Master, Ruler, King, Leader / rule, direct, reign over, run, manage, plan, protect.

Mary knew that God is a powerful, perfect, forever ruler. She trusted him to rule her life.

We know that Jesus is that powerful, perfect, forever ruler. You can trust him to rule your life.

For Older Children

- Why do you think Mary was willing to obey God as her master so fearlessly and whole-heartedly?

Mary knew that God is a powerful, perfect, forever ruler. She trusted him to rule her life.

We know that Jesus is that powerful, perfect, forever ruler. You can trust him to rule your life.

Deeper Discussion Questions

> ⓘ *Use any question(s) you think will best help your group to think and talk about what it looks like to live trusting the perfect, powerful rule of God's forever King. The first two don't assume a personal relationship with God. The final question encourages children who are trusting in Jesus to think about situations in which they might have to act in faith like Mary did.*

- Do you find it hard or easy to have people in charge of you? What would someone have to be like for you to willingly let them rule everything in your life?

- What would you want to know or see or hear in order to trust God as radically and willingly as Mary did?

- Have there been times in your life or the lives of people you know when you have had to trust that:
  - God's ways are right and perfect—even if life seemed hard?
  - God is powerful to do what he has promised—even if it seemed impossible?

Let's Talk to God about That

Here are a number of possible ways of encouraging the children to turn what they have learnt into prayers of praise. Judge which is most appropriate for your group. They move loosely from most supported and least independent to most open and least scaffolded.

1. Say sentences of praise such as the ones below and invite the children to say "WOW!" after each line.

- *Jesus, you are God himself!*

- *Jesus, you will rule over your people for ever!*

- *Your kingdom will be one of goodness, greatness, justice and peace!*

- *Jesus, you are the powerful, perfect, forever King who God promised to send!*

- *Jesus, because you are the powerful King, you are the best possible ruler!*

- *Jesus, because you are the perfect King, we can trust you to rule our lives!*

- *Jesus, because you are the forever King, you will never let us down and you will never leave us!*

2. Discuss how they might finish these prayer sentence-starters and invite them to use them to pray, or use their ideas to pray on their behalf.

- *Perfect, powerful, forever Lord Jesus, we praise you because you…*

- *Promise-making Father God, we praise you because you…*

- *Loving King, we thank you that…*

3. Refer to the pictures or biographical details card from the Isaiah 9 passage. Invite the children to choose a picture/phrase/idea they want to praise and thank God for. Open a time of prayer in which they can do that aloud or in their heads.

4. Ask the children what has most struck them:

- *about God the promise-maker.*

- *about how Jesus is different to other rulers.*

- *about how Mary responded to the angel's message.*

Is there anything that has been new for them or has puzzled, amazed or challenged them? What does it make them want to say to God now? Give them the opportunity to pray individually, either in their heads or aloud.

Let's Get Creative

Minimal resources:

- You'll need paper and coloured pens/pencils. Children could draw Gabriel appearing to Mary. Children who can write could add speech bubbles to each character and come up with a sentence summing up the angel's message and Mary's response.

Resources you may have available:

- You'll need the activity book accompanying *The Christmas Promise*: "Gabriel appearing to Mary" colouring page; and/or the wordsearch page.

- You'll need card, pens, glue, craft jewels/jewel stickers, scissors, stapler, tape. Children make a crown to fit (you could cut crown shapes ahead of the lesson for younger children or print and cut crown templates from the internet) and decorate it, adding the name JESUS and the words "powerful, perfect, forever".

More of a project:

- Children stain paper scrolls with cold tea to make it look like parchment and dry it using hair dryers (set up the area with old newspaper/sheets to protect fixtures and fittings from tea stains!). They can copy out or sum up the promise from Isaiah 9 or you can print that ahead of time onto the paper they will stain.

- Gabriel messengers: Add a face, silver foil armour or a paper robe, and wings to a cardboard tube. Add a speech bubble stuck to the torso with the words "Jesus is God's promised forever King".

- Whole-series project: Print a huge version of the King outline provided as a PDF download. Children help to add the letters for "FOREVER KING" to the uppermost sash. They could write them on directly in a style of their choosing, or you could print/cut letters for them to colour or decorate before sticking them on. They draw pictures or add words around the outside of the outline to represent what they have learned from Isaiah 9 and Luke 2 about God's promised King.

At Home

If you'd like to suggest ways that families could enjoy continuing to think about the lesson in the week:

- For younger children: They could read *The Christmas Promise* together. Perhaps they could have take-home questions along the lines of "What makes Jesus different from all the other kings, queens or rulers there have ever been?" and/or "What makes Jesus such a good King?"

- Families could play Four Square/King Square together and talk about Jesus as the King who will occupy the throne for ever and how/why this makes him better than all other rulers.

- Families could enjoy reading / listening to / watching information about a famous ruler together, talking about their strengths and weaknesses, and comparing them with Jesus, the powerful, perfect, forever King.

- Encourage children to learn a memory verse with their family or carer that proclaims Jesus as the forever King:

"For to us a child is born,
to us a son is given,
and the government will be on his shoulders.
And he will be called
Wonderful Counsellor, Mighty God,
Everlasting Father, Prince of Peace."
(Isaiah 9 v 6, NIV)

SESSION 2
The Rescuing King

The Rescuing King - Prepare Your Heart

 Read Luke 2 v 1-20

- How did the shepherds feel when the angel first appeared, and how did the angel tell them they could feel instead (v 9-10)?

- How did Mary respond to the events of her son's birth (v 19)? What about the shepherds (v 17-18, 20)?

The shepherds reveal to us the difference that the coming of "the Messiah, the Lord" as a baby makes to humanity. We no longer need to live in fear of our Creator, and no longer need to stand before him one day in fear of the judgment that is about to come. Instead, we can live in joyful relationship with him, looking forward to standing before him and hearing him say, *Welcome home, friend.*

The first Christmas was a terrifying event for those shepherds. Why? Because heaven touched earth in their presence, and "the glory of the Lord shone around them" (v 9). And when a human comes into contact with something of the majestic purity of God, terror is the result. No sinful human—and that is every human—can stand, or even survive, in his presence. So it was that Isaiah responded to a vision of God with the words "Woe to me! … I am ruined!" (Isaiah 6 v 5). So it was that those shepherds were "terrified" (Luke 2 v 9). What is surprising is not their initial terror, but that it proved not to be necessary—because the angel who came with the glory of God was there to announce that the shepherds did not need to be afraid, but instead could experience great joy. Why? Because "today in the town of David a Saviour has been born to you: he is the Messiah, the Lord" (v 11).

Jesus was born as the promised rescuing King. He is not only the "Mighty God" of Isaiah 9 v 6 but also the "Prince of Peace". He is the reigning lion *and* he is the sacrificial lamb,

upon whom the Lord has laid the iniquity of us all so that he can give us peace with him (Isaiah 53 v 5).

Here is what turns right terror at the prospect of meeting God into joyful anticipation of meeting him. Here is what the children you teach most need, and what you most need. We can know his love and forgiveness and welcome because Jesus has taken our uncleanness and given us his perfection. The baby who lay in the wooden manger that night had come to be the man who hung on the wooden cross to save us from our sins, so that one day he will sit on his throne and welcome us home.

This gospel message prompts "great joy", now as then. Throughout Luke, joy is the emotional marker of faith in Jesus as rescuing King. (See also Luke 1 v 14; 1 v 44; 19 v 37; 24 v 41; 24 v 52.) And this joy reveals itself as praise of God and proclamation to others. How did the shepherds respond once they had seen the baby? "They spread the word concerning [him]" (2 v 17). Why would they not invite others to discover the joy they had found? And they praised God (v 20). Why would they not praise the one who had sent his Son to bring them peace with him?

If you're unexcited about sharing your faith, or finding that praise comes slowly to you, listen to the angel once more: your sin should leave you terrified of God, but God's Messiah has come to save you, to clean you, to give you life and to draw you close. Dwell on the reality of that—for it will be fuel for great joy, even when you walk through difficult times.

- What would you like to praise God for right now, as you reflect on these verses?

- Who would you like to invite to discover this joy over this Christmas period?

The Rescuing King

God's Word Tells Us...
Jesus is God's promised rescuing King. He is great news!

1. Pray
Let's talk to God before we read the story:

Dear God, please show us why Jesus is *really* good news. Amen.

2. Listen

Read *The Christmas Promise* storybook from this page spread...

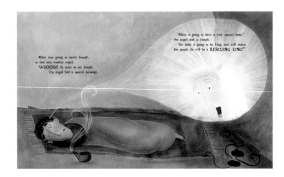

... up to and including the page spread that looks like this, finishing on the left-hand page after the words "just as the angel said":

To make the reading interactive you could:

- ask the children to pretend to be asleep and to wake up when they hear you read "WHOOSH" on the Joseph page.

- invite the children to walk a lap of the room with you, marching along as if they were among the "lots and lots and LOTS of people" on their way to Bethlehem.

- have a go together at making noises for all the different animals you see in the illustration of the manger scene.

- ask the children what sort of beds they and any younger siblings sleep in. What do they think of the idea of sleeping in a feeding box for animals or a mattress of straw?!

- get the children to act out being scared like the shepherds when the angels first appear. Then ask them to act out being super, super happy like the shepherds once they had heard the good news and seen Jesus.

- march around the room again together, this time shouting, "Good news! Good news! Jesus is God's rescuing King!"

3. Thinking
- Did the angels bring the shepherds bad news or good news?

- Did the shepherds find Jesus in a manger, just like the angel said?

- Is Jesus special because he is God's rescuing King?

4. Game

"Rescuing king": If you can source a number of magnetic fishing style games suitable for this age range, have them play in groups to see how many fish they can "rescue" by locating them around the room, picking them up with the rods, and returning them to their "pond" (a bowl or bucket). The children could wear a paper crown to play the role of the rescuing king. An alternative version is for children to take it in turns to run and "rescue" a toy from a bucket and bring it back to their team.

Then say:

"You had to rescue the fishes/toys. You pretended to be a rescuing king! Jesus is God's rescuing King. He came to rescue people."

OR

"Pass the good news": Have inflated balloons (or large, soft balls if you're worried about balloons bursting) on which you draw/ stick a smiley face. Children line up in teams and race to pass the ball along the line and back again. Depending on the age of your kids you could just do it hand to hand or they could pass between their legs / over their heads. Play as many times as they sustain interest! A simpler version could just involve throwing the balls/balloons as far as they can, spreading them about!

Then say:

"The angels gave the good news about Jesus to the shepherds. The good news made the shepherds REALLY happy. And the shepherds gave the good news to other people. Jesus is really good news!"

5. Summary Statement

Jesus is the King who God promised. Jesus is the rescuing King.

6. Listen to God from the Bible

We know this because in the Bible, in Matthew 1 v 21, the angel told Joseph: "[Mary] will give birth to a son. You will name the son Jesus. Give him that name because he will save his people from their sins." (ICB)

7. Pray

Let's talk to God again now:

Lord Jesus, you are the King who rescues your people. You love us so much that you came to save us. Wow! Amen.

8. Craft Ideas

- Give the children the colouring page of the angel and shepherds from the activity book and star stickers (sheep stickers and/or angel stickers too if you can source them) to add to the scene.

- Help the children to make sheep using paper plates/white card circles and cotton wool or curled strips of white paper, black card pre-cut to shape for the head and legs, and stick-on eyes. There are lots of ideas for simple sheep craft online.

- Print / draw copies of the very simple stable scene provided. Provide ink pads / finger paints for the children to dot along the lines of the stables with their finger to colour the scene.

- Help the children to stick yellow strips of paper as hay onto brown card and add a pre-printed-and-cut Jesus figure on top.

As the children enjoy crafting, you could ask them: What was the good news the angels told the shepherds?

God's Word Tells Us...

God promised to send a King who would rescue his people from sin. Jesus is that King. There is no limit to the lengths he will go to—he is the good Shepherd who lays down his life for his sheep.

So What?

The good news is that Jesus transforms fear of judgment into joy and peace with God. A right response involves believing the good news about him, praising him for his rescue, and sharing the good news of who he is.

SECTION	PURPOSE	SUGGESTED ACTIVITY
Let's Get Ready Recap	Recap Session 1.	Children finish a sentence that sums up how Jesus is different to other rulers.
Introduction	Establish the idea that we all need rescuing because we all are like sheep who have turned away from God, our Shepherd. We don't trust, love and obey him as the perfect ruler he is. This is sin, and God punishes sin. We need a rescuer.	"Hunt the lost sheep" activity and brief explanatory talk.
Opening prayer	Pray for the session.	
Let's Hear God's Promise Bible teaching and discussion	Show that God promised to send a rescuer to deal with the problem of sin and judgment. The promised rescuer would die to take the punishment for sin that God's people deserve.	Age-appropriate discussion or Bible study of Isaiah 53 v 6. Both could be done in smaller groups. Note: This section is intended to be a shorter Bible teaching segment than the second one.

🏁	**Let's Play a Game**	Provide a break for concentration. Reinforce the need for or the mechanism of God's rescue mission OR tee up the idea of the transformational power of the good news that turns fear to joy.	Three game options depending on time/space limitations.
📖	**Let's See God's Promise Kept** Bible teaching and discussion	Show from Luke 2 that God kept his promise by sending Jesus: Jesus is the rescuer promised in Isaiah 53. He is good news that transforms fear into joy.	Tell the story of the angel's appearance to the shepherds using Bible verses and interactive story-telling, and involving actors and/or props if possible, drawing out the significance of what the angel says. An example of what this might involve is given below and can be adapted to suit your age group and/or resources.
💬	**What Does This Mean for Us?** Application	Show the different ways in which the shepherds respond to the good news: they trust what they've been told; they go and see; they tell others; they praise and thank God.	Group discussion and guided questions for use as a whole class or in smaller groups.
🙏	**Let's Talk to God about That** Prayer	Give opportunities to talk to God in prayer about any of the different responses they would like to make or think about.	A number of different options depending on the circumstances of the group.
✂️	**Let's Get Creative** Reinforcement	Enjoy an activity together that picks up on an element of the story, giving time for conversation with the children to hear their thoughts about what they've learned.	Craft activities: Various options requiring different levels of resourcing.
🏠	**At Home**	Provide ways for families to continue thinking together about the wonder of God's promised rescuing King.	Various possible activities that pick up on and reinforce this session.

Let's Get Ready

… by looking back at what we learnt about Jesus last week.

- How would you finish this sentence based on last week's Bible passages?
  Jesus is different to every other king there has ever been because…

ⓘ *Do this as a think-pair-share activity, putting any new children in groups with two others who can tell them what they missed.*

Try to draw out the following from last time: Jesus will rule for ever; he will always rule perfectly, with fairness, peace and goodness; unlike other rulers, Jesus is God himself. Children might also say that Jesus is a King promised by God.

Let's Start

ⓘ *Beforehand, print and cut out the pictures of the shepherd and multiple sheep provided and hide the latter all over the room. Hide as many as you think are needed to keep your children occupied for a couple of minutes in hunting them all out. Have some sort of bowl/bucket for them to return the sheep to.*

… by thinking about sheep.

This is a shepherd. His (X number) sheep have turned their backs on him, wandered off, and gone their own way. Now they're in trouble and they can't get back to the shepherd on their own. You need to search for them, rescue them, and bring them back. You have X seconds/minutes to find all the sheep in the room and bring them back to the shepherd. Go!

ⓘ *The children hunt out the sheep against the clock.*

That rescue mission you've just been on is a picture of what we're going to find out about today.

In the Bible, God uses the idea of sheep and their shepherd to explain how people treat God.

God is the perfect ruler of everything and he loves his people. However, instead of loving, listening to and obeying God as their perfect King, people turn their backs on him and try to live life their way. People wander away from God like sheep wandering away from their shepherd. People disobey their rightful ruler. The Bible's word for that attitude to God is sin.

The Bible tells us that sin is serious. It is so serious that God the King will punish that rebellion against him. That is bad news.

But the good news is that God loves his people SO much, that he has a rescue plan for people to save them from the problem of sin. Today we're going to find out how he does that.

Let's Pray

… before we start.

Merciful, loving Father, please show us your amazing rescue plan for people and give us hearts that are thankful for and excited by your promised rescuer. Amen.

Let's Hear God's Promise

We're about to hear another Christmas promise from God's messenger, or prophet, Isaiah. Around 2,700 years ago, Isaiah delivered a promise from God. This promise was about his rescue mission. Isaiah told God's people that God was going to send someone to rescue people from their sin. And he told them HOW.

This rescue mission was so sure to succeed that Isaiah talked about it as if it had already happened. God's promise was so rock-solid certain that instead of saying, "This is how God *will* rescue you…", Isaiah said, "This is how God *has* rescued you"!

For Younger Children

Listen to this line from Isaiah's message and tell me how many people need rescuing.

"We all have wandered away like sheep.
  Each of us has gone his own way." (Isaiah 53 v 6, ICB)

- In Isaiah's words, how many people need rescuing?

We are ALL in trouble. We are ALL like sheep who have wandered away from their shepherd. We are ALL people who have rebelled against the King of the universe. Sin is a problem for ALL of us.

And Isaiah introduces us to the man who can rescue us.

- What do you imagine someone who rescues other people to be like? What are rescuers often like in films? (You could give some examples: Spiderman, Mr Incredible etc.)

Listen to what Isaiah said about that rescuer God promised. See if he sounds strong / a good fighter / like a superhero…

"He was wounded for the wrong things we did.
  He was crushed for the evil things we did.
 The punishment *that brought us peace* was given to him.
  And we are healed because of his wounds." (Isaiah 53 v 5, ICB, italicised phrase from NIV)

- Does God's promised rescuer sound like a mighty warrior to you? Why/Why not?
- How would Isaiah fill in the gap in this sentence?

God's promised rescuer will save us from sin by being _____ in our place. *(Possible answers: killed, punished, crushed, wounded)*

God promised that his rescuing King would save people by facing God's punishment for sin in their place. He would die in order to save people. The Shepherd would die to rescue his sheep.

God's prophet Isaiah doesn't tell us his name. But around 700 years later, a different type of messenger announced that he had arrived.

But before we find out about that… *(Head to "Let's Play a Game" section on the next page.)*

For Older Children

 Do a short Bible study on Isaiah 53 v 4-6, drawing out the universal problem of sin, and God's solution—a promised rescuer who suffers the punishment for sin in place of his people.

The first three questions in the suggested list below recap what has been stated in the introduction, in case those are new ideas for anyone in your group. You may want to talk further about what sin looks like in our lives if you think that would be helpful.

Look up Isaiah 53 v 4-6. Read the verses from God's promise delivered by his messenger Isaiah.

- Which animal are humans compared to in verse 6? *(Sheep)*

- If God is the Shepherd in this word picture, what does the first part of verse 6 say we, like sheep, have done? Put it in your own words. *(A possible summary might be: we have not followed / obeyed / listened to God, the Shepherd. Instead we have gone our own way / tried to be in charge / lived life our own way / rebelled against the ruler.)*

- What does the second part of verse 6 call that disobedience? *(Iniquity, evil, sins, depending on the translation you use)*

- According to verse 6, how many people need rescuing from God's punishment for sin? *(Everyone, all of us, each of us)*

- According to verses 5 and 6, what does the promised rescuer do to save us from having to face God's punishment for sin? *(He was punished / pierced / crushed / wounded, instead of us / in our place.)*

- Does anything strike you or surprise you about this description of God's promised rescuer?

God's promised rescuer would save people by facing God's punishment for sin in their place. The prophet Isaiah doesn't tell us his name. But around 700 years later a different type of messenger announced his arrival.

But before we find out about that…

Let's Play a Game

OPTION 1

ⓘ *A choice of two active games that touch on either the need for or the nature of Christ's rescue mission.*

The first is a familiar game that lets off steam and illustrates being stuck, unable to release yourself and needing a rescuer.

Play Stuck in the Mud/Freeze Tag by appointing someone / a small number of children to be catchers. When they tag an individual that person has to freeze legs apart or arms out and can only be freed by another runner crawling through their legs or ducking under an arm. Play for as long as you want or until all are stuck.

In that game you had to rely on someone else to rescue you when you were stuck. God promised to send a rescuing King who would save us because we can't save ourselves.

We're going to hear about the arrival of God's promised rescuing King now…

ⓘ *Another familiar game involves changing places with others to recap the idea that God's rescuing King saved people by taking their punishment for sin instead of them.*

You need as many seats/spots as there are children. The teacher / game leader calls out "Change places if you… have red hair / are wearing green / go to X school / have a birthday in May etc." and tries to steal the place of one of the people who are in the process of swapping, who then becomes the game leader and calls the next "Change places if…"

That game involved a lot of changing places. God promised that his rescuing King would save his people by suffering God's punishment in their place.

We're going to hear about the arrival of God's promised rescuing King now…

OPTION 2

ⓘ *This is a game about opposites to tee up the idea of the transforming power of the good news to turn fear into joy. If you choose to play this with younger children, you may need to draw/find pictures rather than write the concept for each clue.*

Teams compete in a game of charades in which the correct answer is the opposite of the word acted out. You'll need opposites that are relatively easy to act out and that clearly indicate which word they have to act and which word the team has to give to score the point. For instance, COLD—the correct answer is HOT. Give each team 2 or 3 minutes, with a new member stepping forward to act out a clue once the previous one is correctly guessed each time until the time runs out.

In that game, you started thinking about one thing and ended up talking about the opposite. In the true story from the Bible we're about to read, the people started out feeling one way and ended up feeling the opposite.

Let's See How God Kept His Promise

We're going to hear from God as we read part of Luke's account of the first Christmas again now. We'll see how God showed people that he was keeping his Christmas promise.

ⓘ *Think about ways you can include visuals and/or movement in your New Testament storytelling. This particular passage involves a lot of movement, and children could move about the room with you, travelling from Nazareth to Bethlehem, then to a hillside scene, then to the manger. If you act out the story, children could play the non-speaking parts and a co-leader the role of the angel. The sample script below is based on the ICB and NIRV translations. It imagines you have a narrator, an angel, shepherds, Mary and Joseph and a baby. At various junctures, the action is paused ("Freeze frame!") to allow for comments or whole-group discussion to help draw out the significance. Depending on the age of your children, you may want to create a shorter and simpler version of the story and/or act it out with toy figures.*

Luke chapter 2 tells us that…

Narrator: A Roman Emperor called Augustus sent an order to all people in the countries that were under Roman rule. The order said they must list their names in a register. Everyone went to their own town to be registered.

So Joseph left a town called Nazareth and went to the town of Bethlehem. This town was known as the town of King David. Joseph went there because he was from the family of King David.

Joseph registered with Mary because she was engaged to marry him. She was expecting a baby. While Joseph and Mary were in Bethlehem, the time came for her to have the baby. She gave birth to her first son. There were no rooms left in the inn, so she wrapped the baby with cloths and laid him in a box where animals are fed.

- Freeze frame! We're going to leave Mary and her son for a moment and we're going to go to a different scene.

ⓘ *At this point, choose 3-4 children to sit apart and play the role of the shepherds.*

I want you to imagine you're sitting out under the starry sky. You are huddled up to keep warm. Perhaps you're rubbing your hands together or warming them on a fire. *(Encourage the kids to act these things out.)*

Around you, you can hear the bleating of sheep. *(Distribute toy sheep around them if you have those props available.)*

Perhaps you can feel the warmth of a sheep lying down next to you. That's because you are shepherds, keeping watch over your sheep in the fields near Bethlehem. Maybe you know all about sheep wandering off. Maybe you know all about having to go and rescue them. Maybe you're sitting there in the dark remembering the words of Isaiah 53, when suddenly…

Narrator *[in a booming voice]*: An angel of the Lord stood before them. *[Cue dramatic appearance of a leader dressed as a warrior angel if possible.]* The glory of the Lord was shining around them. They… were… TERRIFIED. *[Encourage the children to really get into character at this point!]*

Angel *[warmly, slowly and clearly]*: Do not be afraid. I bring you good news. It will bring great joy for all the people.

- Freeze frame! How did seeing this display of God's greatness make the shepherds feel to begin with? What word beginning with the letter/sound "j" did the angel say their fear would turn into? Let's act that out: show me fear… show me joy… fear… joy… fear, joy, fear, joy!
  The angel is about to tell the shepherds about some good news that has happened in Bethlehem. This will transform their fear into joy. Listen out for the three names or titles he mentions. Action!

Angel *[slowly and clearly]*: I bring you good news… Today your Saviour was born. He is Christ, the Lord.

- Freeze frame! Which word did the angel use that means the same as "rescuer"? Which name beginning with the word/sound "C" means "God's promised King"? Which name means "God himself"?

Hurray! The forever King who God promised in Isaiah chapter 9 had arrived! Hurray! The rescuer who God promised in Isaiah chapter 53 had arrived!

A round of applause for our actors please!

ⓘ *Ask the actors to go and sit with the rest of the group.*

Did you notice how the arrival of God's promised rescuing King turned everything around?!

The shepherds' first reaction to seeing the glory of God was fear. If we had to face God and explain to him why we hadn't loved and obeyed him perfectly, we would rightly feel very fearful too.

But the angel said that the message of the rescuing King could turn fear into joy.

It all depends on how we respond to the good news.

The shepherds could have shrugged, stayed in the field and acted as if the angel never came. But they didn't. We're going to pick out the different things they did that reveal their response to the good news.

As you listen to what they did:

- point at your head when they show that they believe what the angels have told them.

- point at your eyes when they see Jesus for themselves.

- point at your lips when they tell other people the good news.

- point up when they thank and praise God.

So, four actions (rehearse action for each one): trust, look, tell, praise.

Listen to Luke chapter 2 verses 16-18 and 20: "[The] angels left the shepherds and went back to heaven. The shepherds said to each other, 'Let us go to Bethlehem and see this thing that has happened. We will see this thing the Lord told us about…'" *(Head, trust—they are trusting the angel's promise and taking his words to them as true. Children may also point to their eyes, since "see" is mentioned.)*

"So the shepherds went quickly and found Mary and Joseph. And the shepherds saw the baby lying in a feeding box." *(Eyes, look)*

"Then they told what the angels had said about this child. Everyone was amazed when they heard what the shepherds said to them." *(Lips, tell)*

"Then the shepherds went back to their sheep, praising God and thanking him for everything that they had seen and heard." *(Up, praise)*

What Does This Mean for Us?

We've heard how the shepherds responded to the good news.

- How do you feel about this news?

   Perhaps you feel interested and you want to look at what the Bible says about Jesus and find out more *(point to your eyes as you say this)*.

   Perhaps you believe God's good news and want to say sorry to Jesus and put your trust in him as your rescuing King *(point to your head)*.

   Perhaps you're excited and you want to tell other people *(point to your lips)*.

   Perhaps you're feeling joyful and you want to say "thank you" to God *(point up)*.

We're all going to think now about how we'd like to respond. In a moment, with our eyes closed, we're all going to use our hands to show what we'd like to do next. And if you're not sure whether you want to find out more *(touch eyes)*, tell other people about what you've learnt today *(touch lips)*, thank God *(point up)*, or trust God's promise *(touch head)*, you can just leave your hands in your lap—that's fine too!

So let's close our eyes. Now, think about how you'd like to respond to the good news we've heard today… And let's show God that by doing our action… now.

ⓘ *Think about how you will follow up with children and their parents/carers if any children indicate that they'd like to find out more.*

Deeper Discussion Questions

Use any question(s) you think will best help your group to think and talk about what it looks like to respond to the good news of God's rescuing King. The first set of questions is more appropriate if you're not assuming a personal relationship with Christ. The latter two are more appropriate for children who are already trusting in Jesus as their rescuing King.

- The shepherds went to see Jesus for themselves. What are the different ways you could find out more about Jesus today? How could you get answers to any questions you have about Jesus?

- The shepherds told other people what they had seen and heard. What opportunities do you have to talk about Jesus? What do you find most exciting about Jesus? What do you want to tell your friends and family about him?

- The shepherds praised and thanked God for everything they had seen and heard. What do you think praising and thanking God involves today? What moments are there in your day when you could stop and say "thank you" to God and tell him why he's amazing?

 ## Let's Talk to God about That

ⓘ *Here are a number of possible ways of encouraging the children to turn what they have learnt into prayer. You will need to judge what is most appropriate for your group. They move loosely from most supported and least independent to most open and least scaffolded. Which you choose may depend on how children responded in the last activity.*

1. Use the following to pray on the children's behalf about the four different responses. Tell them to say "yes please" in their heads when they hear something that they want to say to God too.

Father God, we are full of joy and we want to thank you for your kindness in sending Jesus to be the rescuing King who saves us from sin. We think you are a loving Shepherd and we want to tell you you're amazing.

There are other people we want to hear the good news too. We're thinking about their names now. Please help us to tell them all about Jesus and how he rescues his people.

We want to find out more about Jesus for ourselves. Please give us opportunities to discover more about him and get to know him better.

And we want to trust your promises like the shepherds did. Please give us faith to believe in Jesus as our rescuing King.

Amen.

2. Discuss how they might finish these prayer sentence-starters and invite them to use them to pray, or use their ideas to pray on their behalf.

- *Perfect, loving Father God, we're sorry that...*

*   *Lord Jesus, our great Shepherd, thank you for…*

*   *Lord Jesus, our rescuing King, we praise you because…*

3. Ask the children what has most struck them:

*   *about why we need a rescuer.*

*   *about the rescuer God has sent.*

Is there anything that has been new for them or has puzzled, amazed or challenged them? What does it make them want to say to God now? Give them the opportunity to pray individually either in their heads or aloud.

4. Invite older children to turn any of the ideas that came up during discussion into a silent prayer. Anyone who would prefer not to pray could use the time to write down any questions they might have or write their own personal response to what they've heard which they can share or keep private as they choose.

Let's Get Creative

Minimal resources:

*   You'll need paper and coloured pens/pencils. Children could draw and colour one element of the story (the angels' appearance to the shepherds or the shepherds' visit to Jesus). Alternatively they could make a comic strip showing the sequence of action: shepherds in fields; angels' appearance to terrified shepherds; angels' announcement; shepherds set off; shepherds find Jesus; shepherds return full of joy.

Resources you may have available:

*   You'll need the activity book accompanying *The Christmas Promise*: "The shepherds' surprise" drawing pages.

*   You'll need paper or card, pens, staples/glue/tape, scissors, other means of decoration e.g. stickers/glitter. Print the megaphone template provided onto paper/card. Children decorate it with "GOOD NEWS" and "GOD'S RESCUING KING" plus any other adornments of their choice before cutting and rolling and sticking it as a megaphone.

*   You'll need card circles / paper plates, crayons or paper for a range of skin colours, pens, different colours of pen/wool for hair, lolly/popsicle sticks. Children make/draw a face on one paper circle to look terrified and make/draw a face on a second paper circle to look overjoyed. They stick these either side of a lolly/popsicle stick and write on the stick: God's rescuing King is the good news that turns fear into… JOY.

More of a project:

*   You'll need cotton wool or white paint or paper doilies or paper plates, plus black card and stick-on eyes. Choose a sheep craft design from the huge number of simple ideas available online. Children can make a sheep and write or stick on the reverse the words of Isaiah 53 v 6 (ICB):

    *"We all have wandered away like sheep. Each of us has gone his own way.
    But the Lord has put on him the punishment for all the evil we have done."*

- Whole-series project: On the huge version of the King outline provided as a PDF download, children help to add the letters for "RESCUING KING" to the middle sash. They could write them on directly in a style of their choosing, or you could print/cut letters for them to colour or decorate before sticking them on. They draw pictures or add words around the outside of the outline to represent what they have learned from Isaiah 53 and Luke 2 about God's promised King.

 At Home

If you'd like to suggest ways that families could enjoy continuing to think about the lesson in the week:

- For younger children: They could read *The Christmas Promise* together. Perhaps you could give them a take-home question along the lines of "What transformed the shepherds' fear into joy?" and/or "How had God promised Jesus would rescue people?"

- Families could play their own version of opposite charades together and talk about the difference it makes to know Jesus as your rescuing King who takes away our fear of God's judgment and replaces it with joy at knowing him.

- Families could talk about who they'd like to share the good news of God's rescuing King with and pray together for those people.

- Encourage children to learn a memory verse with their family or carer that proclaims Jesus as the rescuing King:

> "We all, like sheep, have gone astray,
> each of us has turned to our own way;
> and the LORD has laid on him
> the iniquity of us all."
> Isaiah 53 v 6 (NIV)

SESSION 3

The New King

The New King – Prepare Your Heart

 Read Matthew 2 v 1-12

- What do we know about the men who show up in Jerusalem, looking for Jesus (v 1-2)?

- What do they know when they turn up, and what don't they know (v 2)?

There is very little detail given about these men! There may be a carol called *We Three Kings of Orient Are*, but we do not in fact know that there were three of them, and they were not kings but rather Magi—probably astrologers who were known for their learning. We also have no real idea from where in "the east" they came from.

Nevertheless, these intriguing men are a key part of the Christmas story, for the one fact that we often miss: they are the only people in the narrative who do not live within the boundaries of Israel. They are outsiders, without access to at least some of the Old Testament (hence they have to ask where the Messiah will be born). And yet they have come to worship the "king of the Jews", and presumably they somehow know that a king different from any other had been promised to the Jewish people—a new kind of king. So while Herod is antagonistic towards the idea that Jesus rules, and while the Jewish religious leaders know the Scriptures but appear indifferent to its fulfilment, it is these outsiders who make the effort to find Jesus, and they alone who bend the knee to him in worship.

And they are right to, because Jesus is a King not just for the Jews but for the world. Only the world is a kingdom large enough for his worth and majesty: "it is too small a thing," God had said through Isaiah, "for [Jesus] to be my servant to … bring back those of Israel I have kept. I will also make [him] a light for the Gentiles, that my salvation may reach to the ends of the earth" (Isaiah 49 v 6).

This is challenging: Jesus will accept no rivals, for he has no equal. But this is also thrilling: Jesus is the one who is King over everyone, and to whom anyone may come. Heaven will be full of people from every tribe and tongue and nation. The kingdom of Jesus covers all corners of the earth, includes anyone who will come to him in faith, and reaches into every aspect of our lives.

The story of the New Testament can be seen as the giving of the nations to King Jesus. By the end of Acts, Jesus' kingdom comprises people of different languages, skin colours and cultures. The subsequent history of the church is part of that same great story too—of people following in the Magi's footsteps to come from the outside and worship the King of the Jews. So we too are part of this great story of God giving the nations to his Son. There is not a single person—and not a single child in your group—to whom Jesus will not say "Welcome" if they come to him on bended knee. It does not matter where they're from, what they've done, or how little of the Bible they know. Whether it's their first time or hundredth time in your group, there is no child who is not invited to worship Jesus.

But before you invite those children to worship, spend time worshipping this forever, rescuing, new King yourself. What will it look like for *you* to kneel at his feet this Christmas—to give him all of who you are and the best of what you have, because you understand that he is a new King and a unique King, and your greatest desire is simply to worship him as *your* King?

- How do you answer that question?

- Could you pray for every child in your group each day of the rest of December, that they would come to worship, or keep worshipping, Jesus as their King?

God's Word Tells Us...
Jesus is God's promised new King. Jesus is King for all sorts of people everywhere.

1. Pray
Let's talk to God before we read the story:

Dear God, please show us why Jesus is a new type of king. Amen.

2. Listen

Read *The Christmas Promise* storybook from the right-hand page on this spread, changing the opening words to, "The shepherds weren't the only ones who had heard the good news about the promised new King…"

… to the end of the book.

Here are a few ideas for how to make the reading interactive:

- darken the room and shine a torch on the wall as the star. Move the "star" around and ask the children to follow it either by pointing or by moving around the room.

- invite the children to walk an excited lap of the room with you, imitating the wise men on their loooong journey

to see the new King. You could wrap some small boxes / empty cardboard tubes as gifts for them to select from and carry on their journey.

- enjoy a brief musical-statues type game that involves bowing down as in the picture when the music stops.

- if appropriate, ask the children where in the world they think the different rulers shown on the penultimate double-page spread come from. Does each one rule all the countries everywhere or just one country each?

- invite suggestions for the King's name before you turn the final page. Get everyone to shout "JESUS" as you turn the page.

- children at the older end of the age-range might be able to suggest why the illustrator has included those four pictures on the final page.

3. Thinking
- Did God send a star to show the wise men where to meet God's new King?

- Did the wise men come all the way from another country to meet God's new King?

- What is the name of God's promised new, forever, rescuing King?

4. Game

"Going on a journey": Set up some sort of obstacle course appropriate to the age of the children. It might involve stepping/jumping in hoops, climbing up and going down a mini-slide, crawling under tables or through a pop-up tunnel etc… If appropriate, they could undertake the "journey" as a race with team members completing the course one at a time.

Then say:

"You just went on a journey, a bit like the wise men. The wise men went on a loooong journey to see Jesus. God sent them to meet Jesus, even though they came from far away."

OR

"All sorts of people": Print and cut out pictures of people from all over the world, or use pre-cut paper figures of all sorts of ethnicities. You could hide lots of them around the room for children to find and bring to put in a bucket with "King Jesus" and a crown stuck on it. Or they could race to collect a person from one side of the room to add to their team's bucket. At the end look at all the different people who have "come" to Jesus.

Then say:

"The wise men showed us that all sorts of people came to meet King Jesus. And in our game all sorts of people from all sorts of places came to King Jesus! In the world today, all sorts of people from all sorts of places love King Jesus."

5. Summary Statement

Jesus is the King God promised. Jesus is the new King for all sorts of people everywhere.

6. Listen to God from the Bible

We know this because in Luke chapter 2 verse 32 the Bible says that Jesus is like "a light to reveal God to the nations" (NLT). Jesus shows God to the whole world.

7. Pray

Let's talk to God again now:

Lord Jesus, you are the King who welcomes all sorts of people from all over the world. You love and look after all different types of people—including us. Wow! Amen.

8. Craft Ideas

- Children make a paper-plate world by sticking on a blue circle of paper and green pre-cut shapes. Provide a crown shape they can decorate and stick to the top of the plate and a note to stick at the bottom saying, "Jesus is the new King. He is King for all sorts of people everywhere."

- Print the tracing activity sheet provided. Older children in the age range could trace with a crayon or do finger painting along the various differently shaped dotted lines (curves, zigzags) between the Magi and Jesus' house.

- Cover one end of cardboard tubes with a dark piece of paper that has a star shape stamped out of it. Children each decorate a cardboard tube using, for example, stickers and/or pre-gummed paper to be a telescope, such that when they look through, they see a star.

- As the children enjoy crafting, you could ask them what makes Jesus such a special King.

God's Word Tells Us...
God promised to send a new type of king who would be for all types of people. Jesus is that King. There is no limit to the extent of his rule—he is the rescuing, forever King for people from every tribe, tongue and nation.

So What?
The good news is that Jesus welcomes all sorts of people from all over the world into his kingdom. A right response is to accept that invitation by recognising and worshipping him as our King.

SECTION	PURPOSE	SUGGESTED ACTIVITY
Let's Get Ready Recap	Recap Sessions 1 and 2.	Children identify and correct errors in sentences that sum up Jesus' identity as God's promised, rescuing, forever King.
Introduction	Establish the idea that earthly rulers only have authority over a particular group of people—the extent of their rule is limited. .	Activity in which the children attempt to match pictures of various seats of power to the country over which they rule.
Opening prayer	Pray for the session.	
Let's Hear God's Promise Bible teaching and discussion	Show that God promised to send a rescuer who would bring salvation from sin not just to the people of Israel, but to "the ends of the earth". He would be a King unlike any other and would be so great that one day even the rulers of the world will all bow down before him.	Age-appropriate discussion or Bible study of Isaiah 49 v 5-7. Both could be done in smaller groups. Note: This section is intended to be a shorter Bible teaching segment than the second one.

Let's Play a Game	Provide a break for concentration. Reinforce the idea that Jesus came to be King for people from all over the world OR introduce the idea of making choices that show what we value most.	Two different game options depending on time/space limitations.
Let's See God's Promise Kept Bible teaching and discussion	Show from Matthew 2 v 1-12 that God kept his promise by sending Jesus: Jesus is the new type of King whose kingdom welcomes people from every nation.	Tell the story of the Magi's visit using Bible verses and interactive storytelling, and involving actors and/or props if possible, drawing out the significance of the Magi's journey in search of the King of the Jews. An example of what this might involve is given below and can be adapted to suit your age group and/or resources.
What Does This Mean for Us? Application	Discuss why this is good news for us: Jesus is the promised, rescuing, forever King for all sorts of people, whatever our age, race, nationality or background. Encourage the children to consider the actions and response to Jesus of the Magi, and what attitude lies behind them.	Group discussion and guided questions for use as a whole class or in smaller groups. (Focusing on the Magi in a passage with many characters provides a clear, positive example of a right response to Jesus. Depending on your group and time, you could also share the verses that tell us Herod's response and consider the heart attitudes and motives that lie behind his rejection of Jesus, but that is not the focus of the material provided.)
Let's Talk to God about That Prayer	Give opportunities to talk to God in prayer about the pictures of Christ and responses to him that they've thought about.	A number of different options depending on the circumstances of the group.
Let's Get Creative Reinforcement	Enjoy an activity together that picks up on an element of the story, giving time for discussing with the children what they think about what they've learned.	Craft activities: Various options requiring different levels of resourcing.
At Home	Provide ways for families to continue thinking together about the wonder of God's new King.	Various possible activities that pick up on or reinforce this session.

Let's Get Ready

… by looking back at what we learnt about Jesus over the last two weeks.

I'm going to say some sentences summing up what we've seen. You need to spot and change any incorrect words in each sentence. Ready?!

- God promised to send a King who would be like all the other kings. *(like/unlike)*

- God promised his King would be all-powerless, and always imperfect, for no time. *(powerless/powerful, imperfect/perfect, no/all)*

- God promised his King would rescue people from sin by dancing in their place. *(dancing/dying)*

- An angel announced the arrival of God's promised King to a young girl called Magda and to some sailors. *(Magda/Mary, sailors/shepherds)*

- Mary doubted God because she knew that he is a perfect, forever ruler. *(doubted/trusted or believed)*

- The shepherds showed us that the good news about Jesus can turn fear into jam. *(jam/joy)*

Let's Start

… by thinking about the rulers of different countries.

ⓘ *Children will attempt to match a government building to the country it serves. Some pictures are included in the downloadable resources. Depending on the age of your children, you could ask them either to try to identify the country from a photo of the building or you could give them the list of countries and ask them to match them up. The key idea is that great power is exercised from those centres of government BUT the authority of each one is limited to its own country.*

- Here are some pictures of government buildings from around the world. Can you tell me which country each one rules over?

The rulers and governments who work in those buildings have a lot of power to serve and lead their countries. BUT they don't have power or authority over other countries. Their rule is only for their people.

We have already seen a number of ways God's promised King is different: he is always perfect; he will rule for ever; and he came to save us from a problem no other ruler can deal with—sin.

Today we're going to think about another way God's promised King is different to and better than all other rulers.

Let's Pray

… before we start.

All-knowing, all powerful Father, please wow us and encourage us with your description of your King who is above all other kings and rulers. Amen.

Let's Hear God's Promise

... and discover how the reign of God's promised King is different to that of other leaders. We're going to look at another section from God's promise made through his messenger Isaiah.

For Younger Children

   ⓘ *You will need a printout of the images provided:*

- *The picture representing God*
- *The picture representing God's promised King*
- *The speech bubbles representing various content from Isaiah 49 v 5-7*

In this passage from Isaiah's writings, it's as if we get to hear a conversation between the Lord God *(put up the picture of the large crown)* and the rescuing King he has promised to send *(put up the picture of a figure wearing a crown)*.

These speech-bubble pictures represent some of the things each one would say. Each time I read a line based on Isaiah chapter 49 verses 5-7, you decide which picture represents what I've just said and who you think said it.

   ⓘ *Put the correct speech bubble by the correct picture after each sentence.*

"The LORD God will honour me and give me strength." (v 5)

   ⓘ *The speech bubble containing the picture of a strong arm with a crown on the muscle goes with the picture representing God's promised King.*

"You will do more than rescue the people of Israel. You will show people all over the world the way to be saved." (v 6)

   ⓘ *The speech bubble containing the picture of the world goes with the picture representing God.*

"I am a servant. I am hated by the people." (v 7)

   ⓘ *The speech bubble containing the picture of someone being mocked goes with the picture representing God's promised King.*

"I have chosen you. Kings and princes and leaders will one day bow down to you." (v 7)

   ⓘ *The speech bubble containing the picture of kings kneeling in front of a greater King goes with the picture representing God.*

God's message through Isaiah tells us that God's promised forever, rescuing King is different from other rulers: he is a rescuer and ruler for people all over the world, not just in one country; and one day all other rulers will bow down before him because he is God's chosen King.

For Older Children

   ⓘ *Do a short Bible study on Isaiah 49 v 6-7. The suggested study below is based on the NLT version. If you use a different translation, you may need to adapt the questions given.*

In this passage from Isaiah's writings, it's as if we get to hear the Lord God speak directly to the rescuer he has promised to send.

- In verse 6, God tells the promised rescuer what his role will be. What will he do, according to verse 6? *Take God's salvation to the ends of the earth (not just to the people of Israel).*

- How does the phrase "ends of the earth" help us understand who the "Gentiles" must be? *The parallel phrase tells us that Gentiles are those from other nations / all people everywhere else; that is, outside Israel.*

- What job description is he also given in the first part of verse 7? *Servant*

- How does that sentence say he will be treated initially? *Despised and rejected*

- What does God say in the rest of verse 7 about how he will be treated in the end? *Kings and leaders will recognise him as a greater King and ruler; they will bow down to him and show him honour.*

- According to what we've just read, what are all the different ways that God's promised rescuing King is different from our country's ruler? *He offers hope / rescue / rules over all nations; other rulers will bow down to him; he is a servant of others, including other rulers.*

Let's Play a Game

OPTION 1

ⓘ *A flexible game that emphasises that God's promised rescuer would bring salvation "to the ends of the earth". Print out one downloadable map of the world per team, and then cut it up, making sure that you have as many or more parts of the map to collect as there will be children in each team.*

Divide the group into at least two teams (if you have more teams, you'll need more cut-up world maps). Teams must complete challenges that you come up with in order to win the different parts of the world; depending on age and/or space those challenges could be riddles to solve, trivia questions to answer, an obstacle/race course to complete, or another physical challenge to perform.

Teams race against one another to "win the world". Their aim is to be the first team to win the entire world, which they do by each individual completing a challenge, one at a time, in order to win part of the map. The first team to correctly reassemble the map wins.

In that game your aim was to gather the whole world. That is what God promised that his rescuing

King would do. He promised that his King would come first to the people of Israel and then take

God's rescue for sin to the whole world so that all sorts of people from all over the world would be part of his kingdom. Let's see him starting to keep that promise in the Christmas story.

OPTION 2

ⓘ *A resources-light game that sets up the idea of devoting ourselves to the things we value.*

Play a variation of "Would you rather…?", perhaps incorporating some sort of physical movement by which the children indicate their choices (run to one side of the room or the other; hands on head, hands on hips…) Make the choices ones in which children have to decide from two options which they would rather devote their time/money/ energies to according to which is personally more valuable to them. For example:

- *Would you rather spend your pocket money on a computer game or a cinema trip with your friends?*

- *Would you rather travel 100 miles to watch (famous sportsperson known to your kids) play or to watch (pop group known to your kids) perform?*

- *Would you rather give money away to a charity that supports X or Y?*

- *Would you rather spend an afternoon reading a book or listening to music?*

- *Would you rather queue through the night to meet (famous person A) or (famous person B)?*

In that game the thing you valued most was the thing you chose. What you valued most was the thing you were willing to devote yourself to.

In the true story we're about to look at, we'll meet a group of people and discover who they valued most—and why.

Let's See How God Kept His Promise

We're going to hear from God as we read part of Matthew's account of the first Christmas. We'll see how Jesus first began to keep the promise God made in Isaiah chapter 49.

ⓘ *Think about ways you can include visuals and/or movement in your New Testament storytelling, especially for younger children. Possibilities include: road signs to the different places mentioned, with movement between them; pictures for different stages of the story; toy figures for the characters; a puppet theatre; a props box for you to pull relevant objects/clothes out of if you are the only leader/actor; leaders dressed up and acting the passage; children travelling around the room to different "scenes" as the characters in the story do likewise. The sample script below is based on the ICB and NIRV translations and could be read by a single narrator or incorporate other leaders or children reading lines for Herod and the Magi. At various junctures, the action is paused ("Freeze frame!) to allow for comments of whole-group discussion to help draw out the significance.*

 Narrator: Jesus was born in a town called Bethlehem during the time when a man called Herod was king.
After Jesus was born some wise men came from the East to the important city of Jerusalem. They came to ask, "Where is the baby who was born to be the King of the Jews? We saw his star when it rose and we have come to worship him."

- Freeze frame!
What clues did you hear that tell us these were visitors from outside the people of Israel? *(They came from the East; they headed for the main city to get help…)*
What did those wise men already know when they arrived in Jerusalem? What didn't they know yet? *(That the King of the Jews had been born. They didn't know where.)*

The wise men were surprising people for God to send to visit his promised King. They had come from far away and, although they knew something important was happening, they didn't know lots of detail.

Let's find out what happened when they reached the end of their journey.

Narrator: The leading priests told Herod that one of God's messengers, named Micah, had said that God's promised King would be born in Bethlehem. Herod sent the wise men to Bethlehem. After the wise men had listened to the king, they went on their way. The star they had seen went ahead of them. It finally stopped over the place where the child, Jesus, was.
When the wise men saw the star, they were filled with joy. They went into the house where the child was and saw him with his mother, Mary.

- Freeze frame! Have you ever visited a very young child? What do grown-ups tend to do when they first meet a little baby or toddler? What sort of gifts do we normally give when someone has a new child?

Let's find out what the Magi did.

Narrator: The wise men bowed down and worshipped the child. They opened their treasures and gave him gifts: gold, frankincense and myrrh.

- Freeze frame! I bet you don't normally see that on a maternity ward! You might not have heard of frankincense and myrrh, but you probably recognise the third treasure that was mentioned—gold.
How would you describe the gifts that the wise men gave Jesus?
What sort of greeting did they give Jesus?
Why did they do both of those things?

Men who had never met Jesus before and who hadn't even known where he was born bowed down before him and gave him their most precious treasures. They did this because they recognised that he is God's King.

The wise men show us that Jesus wasn't born to be King just to the Jews. Jesus was born to be King for all sorts of people from all sorts of places.

What Does This Mean for Us?

I'd like everyone to close their eyes…

And now I want you to try to picture Jesus in your imagination…

It's the run-up to Christmas, so maybe you're picturing a baby in a manger right now. Or you're picturing him with wise men bowing down in front of him. Perhaps you're imagining a carpenter or a man in sandals. Maybe you've got a picture from one of your storybooks in your head.

I'm going to read to you a word picture of Jesus from the book of Revelation that uses special images to help us understand what he is like as a King. I want you to try to imagine it as I read.

"The hair on his head was white like wool, as white as snow. His eyes were like a blazing fire. His feet were like bronze metal glowing in a furnace. His voice sounded like rushing waters. … His face was like the sun shining in all its brightness." (Revelation 1 v 14-16, NIRV)

That power, that beauty, that warmth, that glory… Jesus is THAT King.

Now I want you to imagine a crowd of people around him. What do they look like in your imagination? What language do you imagine them speaking?

You're right if you imagine hearing lots of languages. And you can imagine people of all sorts of nationalities and ethnicities, because Jesus is King for all sorts of people from all over the world—people like Mary, people like the shepherds, people like the wise men, people like us.

Whoever we are, wherever we come from, if we trust Jesus is the new, forever, rescuing King God promised, and if we live treating him as our King, we get to be part of his perfect, forever kingdom.

Open your eyes!

Deeper Discussion Questions

ⓘ *Use any question(s) you think will best help your group to think and talk about what it means to live for and worship Christ as our personal Lord and King. In each case there is an option aimed more at children who would call themselves followers of Jesus and an option that doesn't assume faith and gives room for open expression and discussion of their ideas/responses.*

The wise men only saw a child. But they still treated him as a King. Let's think about what we can learn from their example.

The wise men bowed down to show they recognised Jesus as a King.

- What do you think it looks like for us today to live in a way that shows we know Jesus is our King? OR
  How do you think you would recognise someone who loves and serves Jesus as their King?

The wise men gave Jesus the best treasures they had because they recognised how valuable he is.

- We don't have much in the way of gold, frankincense or myrrh! What do we have that we can choose to dedicate to Jesus because we know he is more valuable than anything else? OR
  Today, people who love Jesus are willing to give up their time, their comfort, their money, even their lives to serve him and tell other people about him. What do you think about that?

The wise men were willing to undertake a potentially long and difficult journey to worship Jesus the King.

- What difficulties might we have to choose to face in order to serve Jesus as our King? OR
  Who would you willingly undertake a difficult journey just to meet? If you had the opportunity to meet Jesus of Nazareth face-to-face, would you want to? Why/Why not?

 ## Let's Talk to God about That

ⓘ *Here are a number of possible ways of encouraging the children to turn what they have learnt into prayer. You will need to judge what is most appropriate for your group. They move loosely from most supported and least independent to most open and least scaffolded.*

1. Say sentences of praise such as the ones below and invite the children to say "WOW!" after each line.

- *Father God, Jesus is your new, forever, rescuing King. You have kept all your amazing promises!*

- *Jesus, we can trust your good rule, enjoy your loving rescue, and be welcomed into your perfect kingdom!*

- *Jesus, your kingdom will be full of all sorts of people from all over the world!*

- *Jesus, you invite all sorts of people, including people like us!*

- *Jesus, you are glorious, powerful and beautiful!*

- *Jesus, you are worth following with all our efforts, you are worth worshipping with all our lives and you are worth serving with all our hearts!*

2. Discuss how they might finish these prayer sentence-starters and invite them to use them to pray, or use their ideas to pray on their behalf.

- *Lord Jesus, ruler of the whole world, we praise you that…*

- *Lord Jesus, light to all nations, we thank you that…*

- *Lord Jesus, King of our lives, please help us to…*

3. Refer to the pictures from the Isaiah 49 activity or remind them of the picture of King Jesus we heard described in Revelation. Invite the children to choose something about what Jesus is like and/or what he has made possible that they'd like to praise him for. Alternatively put up a world map such as the one used in the game and invite the children to choose particular countries/people groups to pray for. Open a time of prayer in which they can pray aloud or in their heads.

4. Ask the children what has most struck them:

- *about the descriptions of Jesus they have heard today*

- *about who Jesus came to invite into his kingdom*

- *about the wise men's response to God's new King.*

Is there anything that has been new for them or has puzzled, amazed or challenged them? What does it make them want to say to God now? Give them the opportunity to pray individually either in their heads or aloud.

Let's Get Creative

Minimal resources:

- You'll need paper and coloured pens/pencils. A small number of children could be tasked with drawing pictures of the Magi first spotting and studying the star, and preparing for their journey; the majority of the children draw pictures of them on their journey; a further small number of children draw scenes depicting them making enquiries in Jerusalem, arriving at the house, bowing in worship, or presenting gifts. Lay all the pictures on the floor across the room in order of the story such that the majority of the line is composed of journey pictures. Ask the children why the wise men chose to make the journey.

Resources you may have available:

- You'll need the activity book accompanying *The Christmas Promise*: the wise men wordsearch and the "new king, rescuing, forever king" colouring page.

- You'll need lolly/popsicle sticks, string/thread, glue: the children make a star-shaped Christmas tree ornament (easy instructions are readily available online), writing on the lolly/popsicle sticks "Jesus is the promised King for all sorts of people from all over the world" on one side, and decorating the other with pens / glitter / any other resources.

- Pebble painting: children paint a pebble with dark blue paint before adding a black ground and black figures for the Magi walking silhouetted against the sky and a white/gold star for them to follow.

More of a project:

- Make your own Advent candle: provide children with a table candle and appropriate fine-nibbed multi-surface paint pen. According to the number of days left until Christmas, devise a sentence summarising what the children have learnt. The children write the words in order at regular intervals down the side of the candle such that it will burn down to the next word each day. An example sentence might be, "Jesus is God's promised new, rescuing, forever KING" (adapt to increase/decrease word count as needed). Then they can add further decoration as they wish.

- Whole-series project: On the huge version of the King outline provided as a PDF download children help to add the letters for "NEW KING" to the third sash. They could write them on directly in a style of their choosing, or you could print/cut letters for them to colour or decorate before sticking them on. They draw/add pictures or add words around the outside of the outline to represent what they have learned from Isaiah 49 and Matthew 2 about God's promised King.

At Home

If you'd like to suggest ways that families could enjoy continuing to think about the lesson in the week:

- For younger children: They could read *The Christmas Promise* together. Perhaps they could have take-home questions along the lines of "Who is Jesus King for?" and/or "What did the wise men show us about how to treat King Jesus?"

- Families could play "Would you rather?" and talk about what choices the wise men made and what they knew about Jesus that led them to make those choices.

- Families could choose a country of the world and pray together for Christians in those countries and for people there who don't yet know Jesus as their rescuing, forever King.

- Encourage children to learn a memory verse with their family or carer that proclaims Jesus as the King for all sorts of people everywhere:

"I will also make you a light for the Gentiles,
that my salvation may reach to the ends of the earth."
Isaiah 49 v 6 (NIV)

FAMILY SERVICE

The Forever, Rescuing, New King

The Forever, Rescuing, New King

Summary of Key Message from the Sunday School Lessons...

God promised to send a King unlike any other. Jesus is that King. He is the forever, rescuing, new King.

There will be no limit to the length of his righteous reign. There is no limit to the lengths he will go to to rescue. There is no limit to the extent of his rule.

The good news is that he is the best ruler we could ever hope for: he will be all-powerful and always perfect for all time; he is the good Shepherd who lays down his life for his sheep; and he is all this for people from every tribe, tongue and nation.

Therefore, he is the King who we can trust and entrust ourselves to. He is the King who we can access and come to, whoever we are. He is the King who is worthy of being sought and celebrated and shared and worshipped.

Aims for This Service

- To share with the wider congregation and any visitors what the children have been looking at in Sunday School: to see in passages from Isaiah, Luke and Matthew that Jesus is the promised forever, rescuing, new King.

- To encourage regulars and visitors alike to consider the limitations of earthly leaders and why God's promised King is the best possible ruler.

- To show from the responses of Mary, the shepherds and the wise men that Jesus is a King who can and should be trusted, sought and worshipped.

SECTION	PURPOSE	SUGGESTED CONTENT
Introduction	Think about worldly rulers, including their limitations: they don't last for ever; none is perfect; their power/authority has limited scope, both geographically and in terms of changing people's hearts.	An interactive game/quiz suitable for a range of ages, followed by a brief introduction. A suggested quiz is given below.
Recap: the promise	Briefly articulate three promises God made in Isaiah about a future King he would send.	Visual aids accompanying a brief reading and explanation of each promise in Isaiah. Suggestions for props that could be placed in gift boxes for children to come and pull out are given below.
Short Talk for Adults Optional	Encourage those present to consider why God's promised King trumps all earthly rulers.	A brief talk, directed more towards adults, showing why a righteous, eternal, self-sacrificing, all-welcoming ruler is good news. Bullet points of key ideas and an example talk are included below. *This segment can be omitted without affecting the flow of the service. See further comments in the relevant section below.*
Recap: the fulfilment	Hear from three nativity characters who met Jesus about how Jesus was the fulfilment of Isaiah's promises.	A simple drama: adults dressed up in character as Mary, a shepherd and a wise man each giving a brief summary of their "part" in the Christmas story to a fourth adult, and explaining how Jesus was shown to be the King God promised. A possible script is provided below.
Application/Response	To show what responses of faith in the promised King look like based on those of Mary, the shepherds and the Magi.	Whole-congregation activity in which they have to match a Bible verse to the nativity character it's about. Those characters each articulate a right response to the Christ, before an appeal to consider Christ your King this Christmas closes the teaching part of the service. A possible script is provided below.

⌖ DETAILED OUTLINE

Welcome and Opening Prayer

Introduction

> ⓘ *You will need: 4-6 pictures of various rulers/monarchs from around the world and throughout history, and pictures of flags of the countries they ruled over. Make at least two readily recognisable to kids aged 5-12. (Your Sunday-school leaders may already have pictures they used available.) Try to pick one leader who, in your national context, divides opinion—who some love and some really do not! You'll need to know how long each ruled for.*
>
> *These could be pictures projected electronically; or, if you want to involve much younger children who might struggle to contribute to the actual discussion, hide physical pictures around the room for them to find and bring to the front and stick/hold up ready for you to introduce the quiz.*
>
> *Introduce a family quiz in three rounds, giving a minute for each discussion:*

1. In your family group / with those around you, can you work out which leader/monarch ruled over which country and match their picture to the flag?

2. Can you put them in order from who ruled the longest to who ruled the shortest time?

3. Which do you think was the best of those leaders? Who was the worst?

> ⓘ *Run through the answers after rounds 1 and 2 of the quiz. For stage 3, rather than gathering answers, point out that some rulers do good jobs, some clearly do terrible jobs, and some divide opinion. Then introduce the focus of your time together:*

Throughout history there have been famous rulers. Some of them ruled for many decades. Some ruled for only a few years. Some ruled just for months, weeks or even days!

Some ruled over one country. Some ruled over huge empires.

Some of them are famous for great deeds and good character. Some of them are famous for what terrible rulers they were.

But as we look back over history, we see one ruler after another after another. Rulers come and rulers go. No king or queen lives for ever!

Not only that, but all rulers have limits on their power: no ruler's kingdom has ever included people in every continent.

And however good a ruler has been, however much they change laws or education or healthcare, they can never change people's hearts—including their own.

None of our rulers has ruled perfectly, for everyone, for all time.

BUT, long ago, centuries before the first Christmas, God made a promise. He promised to send a King who would be unlike any other ruler there has ever been.

In Sunday groups over the last three weeks, the children have been learning all about that King— God's promised new, rescuing, forever King.

Today we're going to think about why God's promised King is different to and better than all other rulers.

Song

Recap: the promise

> ⓘ *You will need: four gift boxes/gift bags, each containing one of the following props:*
>
> *1. A scroll with a label attached to it saying "Isaiah"*
>
> *2. A baby doll with the four names for the promised King from Isaiah 9 v 6 written on its vest/Babygro*
>
> *3. A toy sheep*
>
> *4. A globe*
>
> *Invite a child who you know has been in Sunday school to pull an item from the relevant box/bag and tell everyone what it is. After items 2-4, also invite the child to read out the relevant verses from Isaiah, while simultaneously showing them on a screen if possible. Then, after each one, explain the significance of that prop. There is a suggested script below.*

1. SCROLL: Long ago, God promised to send a King. His promised King would be different to all the other rulers there have ever been. Lots of those promises about God's King are found in the book of Isaiah. Isaiah was a messenger who delivered messages from God.

Over the last three weeks, the children have been looking at some of those promises in Isaiah to discover what this promised King is like.

2. BABY: In Isaiah 9 v 6-7 God promised to send a baby boy to be King. God gave him four special names. Those names tell us what the King would be like: he would be full of God's wisdom; he would be the all-powerful God himself; he would rule for ever; he would bring peace. God's promised King would be the **forever King** who will be all-powerful and always perfect for all time.

3. SHEEP: In Isaiah 53 v 5-6 God said people are like lost sheep. This helps us understand what it means to sin against God: God is like a loving Shepherd. We are like sheep who ignore him, wander off and try to live our own way. God promised a King would come to save his "sheep" from God's punishment for sin. God's promised King would be a **rescuing King** who would die in place of lost sheep so that they could be forgiven.

4. GLOBE: In Isaiah 49 v 6-7 God said that his promised King wouldn't be the forever, rescuing King for just one country. He wouldn't just be the forever, rescuing King for a group of countries. God's promised King would be the forever, rescuing King for people from all over the earth! God's promised King would be a **new King** for people from every tribe, language and nation.

Song

Short Talk for Adults

ⓘ *These are the main points for a very short talk aimed primarily at adults, and especially any guests. It adds an opportunity to consider how the promises God made through Isaiah speak to the desires we all have of life and of our leaders, before seeing in the next section of the service that Jesus is the ultimate fulfilment of those longings. If time is limited, or if you want to keep focusing purely on the children, this section could be omitted without affecting the flow of the service.*

- Share some examples of key things we tend to long for in life and for our leaders to deliver or promote: security, freedom, peace, integrity, compassion, skill, and so on.

- Point out the challenges of trying to secure those things for ourselves and the problem with relying on other people who are just like us to do it.

- There is a desire in each of us for someone to put things right—for a perfect ruler. That's because that's what we're made for.

- That's the sort of ruler and rule described in Isaiah 9 v 6—power combined with integrity, offering lasting peace and security.

- He's a ruler unlike any other—for everyone, for ever, fixing problems no one else can, including the problems of our own heart.

- If we look at the world and see a mess—if we look inside ourselves and see a mess—the promised King is good news.

- And even better news: he's already come.

ⓘ *Here is a possible talk script…*

What do you want from life? Maybe a job or promotion, a holiday, a particular school place for your child? What if I asked you for big headlines? What would you say, then? Safety and security? Peace and prosperity? Freedom from want or fear? To know that the world will be safe and peaceful—and stay that way? Perhaps your longings are much closer to home. For peace in your heart. For freedom from anxiety or shame…

And what do you want from the leaders whose actions and decisions affect so many areas of your life? Ability combined with compassion? Leaders who are accessible, who listen, who genuinely care? Leaders who will put your interests ahead of their own? If we ever find such a leader, let's hope they stick around! Not retire, or go after a better offer, or succumb to illness or infirmity.

Here's another question: Do you fancy being that leader? Is that a job description you think you could live up to?!

Often we think we'd do a better job than our leaders at running the nation's life. And we instinctively tend to think we know best out of anyone how to run our own life. Yet I suspect something in us still longs for someone who could secure for us the life we long for ourselves.

According to the Bible, that's because we were designed to live under a King. But if you recoil at that idea, we're not talking about a constitutional monarch like in the UK, or a 14th-century power-hungry monarch intent on securing their own power and cruelly subjugating their own people in order to do so.

We're talking about a King who, as Isaiah 9 v 6 puts it, reigns with "justice and righteousness". A King who offers "greatness of … government and peace". And not just for a season or even only a century, but of whose perfect, loving, life-giving rule "there will be no end".

And this isn't a King who is only interested in a certain territory or race of people. He's a King, as Isaiah 49 puts it, who will take God's salvation and offer of a place in his perfect, forever kingdom "to the ends of the earth".

And he's a King who can fix the things your Prime Minister/President can never fix: the impatience or anxiety or anger or fear or shame or hurt or harm that reside in or come out of your heart.

There is no limit to the length of that King's perfect reign. There is no limit to the type of people he invites to live in his kingdom. There is no limit to what he was willing to go through for your sake.

If you've realised today you long for someone to sort the mess out—the mess out there in the world, and the mess in here in your own heart, there is double good news: firstly, God promised just such a King; and secondly, that King has come…

Song

(i) *If the Christmas story will be unfamiliar for many in your audience, rather than singing together at this stage, you could show a short video of the Christmas story that has been filmed/animated for children. Links to some examples are included in the free download material.*

📖 Recap: the Fulfilment

(i) *You will need: the scroll, baby, sheep and globe props from earlier on; and four adults to play Mary, a shepherd and a wise man (all three of these should be dressed up), and an adult who links things together. After the song or video, the actors could launch straight into this script.*

Adult: holding the Isaiah scroll, he/she reads a bit, looks around, reads a bit more, looks at his/her watch, reads a bit more, looks at watch again, gets fed up of waiting, finally huffs a bit. The other three are entering as this happens.

Mary [holding baby]: Are… are you ok? You seem a bit put out?

Adult: Oh, yes, fine. Just waiting… and waiting. You know how it is when you're looking forward to something. It's like December—it feels like the loooooongest month EVERRRRR as you wait for Christmas.

Shepherd [holding sheep]: Is that what you're waiting for? Because if it is, I've got good news for you: it's only XX days away!

Adult: No, actually I'm waiting for something else. Or someone else, I should say. I've been reading some promises that God made about sending a forever, rescuing King for all types of people and, well, he sounds amazing. I'm just wondering when he will show up. [Checks watch and looks around again.]

[Mary, shepherd and wise man share a glance.]

Wise man [holding globe]: Um…if that's who you're waiting for, then we've got REALLY good news for you.

Shepherd: Those promises you've been reading—they've already come true.

Adult: Wait, what?! When? How? WHO?

Shepherd: We've all met the promised King. Mary was the first, weren't you?

Mary: Yes. The first time I realised God was keeping his promise was when I met an angel. Yeah, really! He came to tell me that I was going to have a son unlike any other child. A son born by God's Holy Spirit. A baby boy called "the Son of the Most High" who would reign for ever and ever. A forever King.

Adult [points excitedly and open-mouthed at the scroll]: Just like Isaiah said!

Mary: Exactly. I told a historian called Luke all about it and he wrote it down in what he called his Gospel, so you can read more about it if you like.

Shepherd [to Mary]: Hey, I met Luke too! Nice guy! [To adult] I was telling him how we—my shepherd friends and I—first found out that God had kept his promise. An angel appeared to us too while we were looking after the sheep [strokes prop]. He told us that a baby had been born in Bethlehem who would be our Saviour—our rescuing King. So, as you can imagine, we rushed off to see him!

Adult [to wise man]: How about you? You've met him too?

Wise man: Yes, when he was a little bit older. I visited him with a group of my friends. God sent a star to guide us to him. Even though we'd come from outside Israel [spins globe], God invited us to meet his King for all nations.

Adult [rolls up scroll]: This is amazing! God kept his promises! That new, forever, rescuing King has already come! I have to go tell everyone! [Starts to rush off. Stops and turns back and says, slowly:] Wait, hang on. What's his name?

[Mary, shepherd and wise man all turn towards kids in the audience and motion for them to answer with them…] On three? One…two…three…

All [hopefully!]: JESUS!

[Adult rushes off. The other three characters remain nearby, ready for the next section.]

Song

Application/Response

The good news is that Jesus is the new, rescuing, forever King who God promised.

The people who first met him show us what it looks like when we ask Jesus to be *our* King.

In a moment, I'm going to read you something the Bible says about each of these three people—Mary, the shepherd and the wise man—and you need to show me who you think it's talking about by doing the right action. Mary's action is like this *[make action of rocking a baby]* as she looks after baby Jesus. The shepherd's action is like this *[place hand on forehead, shielding eyes and looking around]* as he keeps an eye on his sheep. The wise man's action is like this *[march on the spot]* as he travels to see Jesus.

Let's practise those. Everyone stand up… and show me the action for Mary. Shepherd. Wise man. Mary. Wise man. Shepherd… Ok, we're all set.

Who do you think this verse is about…?

- Luke chapter 2 verse 16-17 says, "So [they] went quickly and found Mary and Joseph. And [they] saw the baby lying in a feeding box."

[Pause for everyone to make the correct action…]

Shepherd: Yes, that was us! If you were told that the rescuing King was willing and waiting to meet *you*, you'd want to check it out for yourself, wouldn't you?!

- Matthew chapter 2 verse 11 says, "On coming to the house, they saw the child with his mother Mary, and they bowed down and worshipped him. Then they opened their treasures and presented him with gifts of gold, frankincense and myrrh."

[Pause for everyone to make the correct action…]

Wise man: That was my friends and me! We're talking about the King of the universe! We bowed down to show him that we know he is the King. And we gave him our most precious treasures to show him how special we think he is!

- Luke chapter 1 verse 38 says, "I am the Lord's servant [this person said to the angel]. Let this happen to me as you say!"

[Pause for everyone to make the correct action…]

Mary: Yes, that was me. I know God is powerful. I know God keeps his promises. And because I know God is powerful, promise-keeping and always good, I know I can trust him to rule my life.

ⓘ *This final part is aimed—in content and language—more at the adults in the room.*

Jesus is the King who invites us to know him—the King we can turn back to and trust in for forgiveness, whoever we are.

Jesus is the King who invites us to follow him—the King who is worth seeking and worshipping and devoting our lives to.

Jesus is the King who invites us to trust him—the King we can rely on both to save us and to rule us perfectly. We can entrust our lives and our future to him.

I'd love to ask you, who are you most like as you sit here today? Are you a bit like the shepherds? Do you want to find out about Jesus for yourself? We'd love to invite you to look into who Jesus is, why he came and died and rose by… *[Give details of ways they can do that in your context.]*

Are you like the wise men? Have you realised that Jesus is King—King of everything and everyone, and that he offers you forgiveness for wandering away from him? We'd love to invite you to turn to him and ask him to forgive you and give you faith to trust in and follow him. You could speak to him right now, while I'm talking, but if you'd like to meet up and talk after the service… *[Give details of someone they could talk to after the service.]*

Are you like Mary? Are you already trusting in God's promises for your forgiveness, for life now, and for your forever future? We'd love to invite you to talk to him in your heart as we pray in a moment and ask him to work in you and your life and through you for his good, Jesus-centred, everlasting purposes.

Prayer

Notices, etc.

Song

Closing Words

Other Ideas

- If your church has permission to take photos/videos of children in their Sunday-school groups, you could show a rolling montage of snaps/clips from the three Sunday-school lessons on a big screen as people arrive.

- As you adapt the suggestions above for your context, you might want to get everyone playing one of any silly games that children have played in Sunday school as a fun way of creating a festive atmosphere.

- If the Sunday-school classes wrote on and decorated a large version of the mystery King figure with the kingly sashes provided as a free download, you might want to put that on display.

- Choose songs that are more likely to be familiar to guests and/or are easy to pick up and sing with gusto! Are there songs known to your church family with actions for children to join in with even if they don't know and can't read the words? (Familiar songs and Christmas hymns will vary by country and church, but if you can select such songs that also reflect the focus at that particular point in the service, it can help reinforce the idea.)

 Take-Home Ideas

- A take-home gift of a memory verse (such as Isaiah 9 v 6) provided as (for example) a bookmark or a tree decoration.

- A copy of *The Christmas Promise* for guests with young children.

- A copy of *The Christmas Promise* Colouring and Activity book.

- Material and instructions for a simple take-home craft—see ideas in the "Let's Get Creative" sections of the pre-school and 5-12s sessions.

- Details of, or the link to, a play-list of children's and/or Christmas songs that point to Jesus as God's promised, forever, rescuing King.

Meet the Rest of the Family

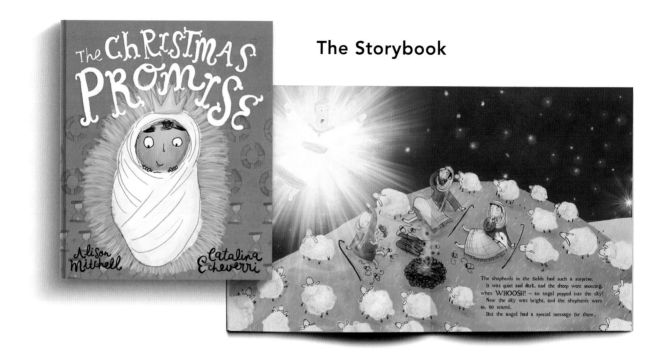

The Storybook

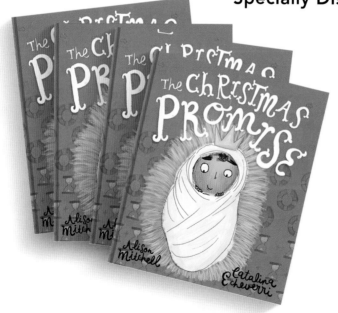

Specially Discounted Ministry Packs

You can buy ministry packs of all these resources at special discounts to enable you to give them to children at your church.

Head to the downloadable resources page and enter your passcode (see page 6) to find out more:

www.thegoodbook.com/tcplessonresources

Advent Calendar and Family Devotional

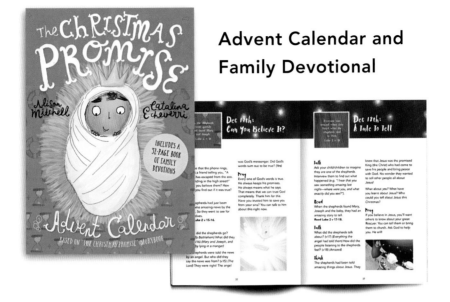

Activity Book

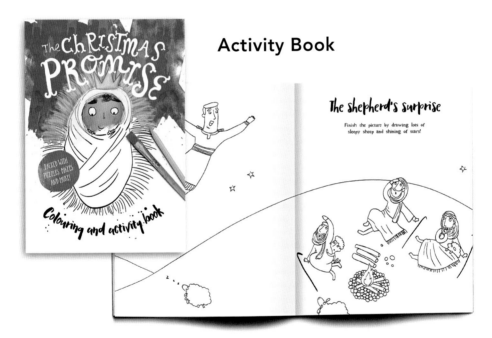

Board Book

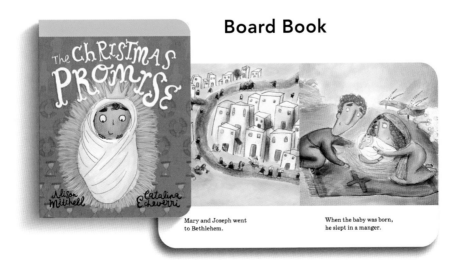